THE HAMLYN LECTURES

TWENTY-SIXTH SERIES

ENGLISH LAW—
THE NEW DIMENSION

AUSTRALIA
The Law Book Company Ltd.
Sydney : Melbourne : Brisbane

CANADA AND U.S.A.
The Carswell Company Ltd.
Agincourt, Ontario

INDIA
N. M. Tripathi Private Ltd.
Bombay

ISRAEL
Steimatzky's Agency Ltd.
Jerusalem : Tel Aviv : Haifa

MALAYSIA : SINGAPORE : BRUNEI
Malayan Law Journal (Pte) Ltd.
Singapore

NEW ZEALAND
Sweet & Maxwell (N.Z.) Ltd.
Wellington

PAKISTAN
Pakistan Law House
Karachi

ENGLISH LAW—
THE NEW DIMENSION

BY

LESLIE SCARMAN

A judge of the Court of Appeal

Published under the auspices of
THE HAMLYN TRUST

LONDON
STEVENS & SONS
1974

First Impression 1974
Second Impression 1975
Third Impression 1977
Fourth Impression 1978

Published by Stevens & Sons
Limited of 11 New Fetter
Lane in the City of London
and Printed in Great Britain by
Lewis Reprints Ltd., London
and Tonbridge

SBN Hardback 420 44690 7
Paperback 420 44700 8

CONTENTS

THE HAMLYN LECTURES

THE HAMLYN TRUST

The Hamlyn Trust came into existence under the will of the late Miss Emma Warburton Hamlyn of Torquay, who died in 1941 at the age of eighty. She came of an old and well-known Devon family. Her father, William Bussell Hamlyn, practised in Torquay as a solicitor for many years. She was a woman of strong character, intelligent and cultured, well versed in literature, music and art, and a lover of her country. She inherited a taste for law, and studied the subject. She also travelled frequently on the Continent and about the Mediterranean, and gathered impressions of comparative jurisprudence and ethnology.

Miss Hamlyn bequeathed the residue of her estate in terms which were thought vague. The matter was taken to the Chancery Division of the High Court, which on November 29, 1948, approved a Scheme for the administration of the Trust. Paragraph 3 of the Scheme is as follows:—

" The object of the charity is the furtherance by lectures or otherwise among the Common People of the United Kingdom of Great Britain and Northern Ireland of the knowledge of the Comparative Jurisprudence and the Ethnology of the chief European countries including the United Kingdom, and the circumstances of the growth of such jurisprudence to the intent that the Common People of the United Kingdom may realise the privileges which in law and custom they enjoy in comparison with other European Peoples and realising and appreciating such privileges may recognise the responsibilities and obligations attaching to them."

From the first the Trustees decided to organise courses of lectures of outstanding interest and quality by persons of eminence, under the auspices of co-operating universities or other bodies, with a view to the lectures being made available in book form to a wide public.

The Twenty-Sixth Series of Hamlyn Lectures was delivered in December 1974 by Sir Leslie Scarman at the School of Oriental and African Studies in the University of London.

J. N. D. ANDERSON,
Chairman of the Trustees.

December 1974

PREFACE

THE terms of the Hamlyn Trust, so familiar to my audience, have a confident ring—as befits a scheme drafted within three years or so of the vindication of the rule of law by force of arms. Their self-confidence is now somewhat dated: but their reference to the privileges which in law and custom the common people of the United Kingdom "enjoy in comparison with other European peoples" should not blind us to their wisdom: the object of the charity is the furtherance of the knowledge of the comparative jurisprudence of the chief European countries, including the United Kingdom so that we may recognise our responsibilities and obligations. I hope that by the time I have finished I will have dispelled any lingering sense of complacency in my audience and provoked a measure of thought as to the responsibilities of lawyers in the new society that has developed since 1948, when the Trust's Scheme was approved.

LESLIE SCARMAN

December 1974

PART I

INTRODUCTION

MY purpose in these lectures is to attempt an answer to one question: Is English Law capable of further growth within the limits of the common law system?—or, to put the same question in other words—Has the common law reached the end of the road? Of course the question assumes that a meaning can be attached to the phrase "common law system," and that it is possible to distinguish change which develops and strengthens the system from change which destroys it.

I shall endeavour to show that there are in the contemporary world challenges, social, political, and economic, which, if the system cannot meet them, will destroy it. These challenges are not created by lawyers; they certainly cannot be suppressed by lawyers: they have to be met either by discarding or by adjusting the legal system. Which is it to be?

The common law knows as little of its birth as you and I know of ours. It has grown, like Topsy: it is as natural in the English scene as the oak, the ash, and the elder. It antedates Parliament and the legislative process. We cannot point to any body of learned men sitting around a table and designing the law and the system. It is customary law developed, modified, and sometimes fundamentally redirected by the judges and the legal profession working through the medium of the courts. Thus

1

it is, in essence, a lawyer's law. Further, it is lawyers' law of universal application. The common law has, in theory, no gaps or omissions, only a few silences which at any time, upon the instigation of a litigant, the voice of the judge can break. For instance, the common law was exceedingly taciturn for centuries on the subject of the duty of care and the tort of negligence. Pressurised by the developing industrialisation and urbanisation of society in the nineteenth century, the judges, using as a precedent the ancient action on the case, developed the substantive law of negligence, thereby without the intervention of the Parliamentary legislative process providing a legal right to compensation for personal injuries caused by the fault of another. An older and more famous illustration of the same process is the history of equity—developed by the judges as a graft upon the property law, who thus adapted the law to the needs of the time without the necessity of destroying it.

As everyone knows, the common law with its equitable gloss, although a deeply revered heritage of the people, did not by its own process of development, meet all the challenges of change in society. The remedy had to be found by Parliament which evolved the legislative process, passing into law its own statutes. For a time lawyers were disposed to claim the right to challenge the validity of Acts of Parliament. In 1610 (*Doctor Bonham's* case, 8 Co.Rep. 118a) Sir Edward Coke C.J. roundly declared that " the common law will control Acts of Parliament, and sometimes adjudge them to be utterly void." But the temptation soon vanished, sup-pressed effectually by the power of Parliament speaking with the authority of the sovereign and the consent of the Lords and the Commons. Notwithstanding the great volume in modern times of statute law (*e.g.* in 1971 there were enacted 81 Public General Acts covering 2110 pages: the current size of the Statute Book is something like 43,000 pages), the common law survives as the basis of the English legal system. The distinctive juristic feature of the system is the relationship of this customary law, by which I mean the principles of com-mon law and equity declared, developed, and applied by the judges, to statute law, by which I mean the law enacted, or deriving from enactment, by Parliament. The modern English judge still sees enacted law as an excep-tion to, a graft upon, or a correction of, the customary law in his hands: he gives unswerving loyalty to the enacted word of Parliament, but he construes that word strictly, in its statutory context, and always upon the premise, usually unspoken, that Parliament legislates against the background of an all-embracing customary law. There is theoretically no need, and, therefore, no justification, for judges to fill in " gaps " in an Act of Parliament; indeed, such judicial repair of the statute law has been declared by Lord Simonds to be a " naked usurpation of the legislative function under the thin dis-guise of interpretation " (*Magor Rural District Council* v. *Newport Borough Council* [1952] A.C. 189 at page 191). The principle of our law is simply that " if a gap is disclosed, the remedy lies in an amending Act " (page 191).

Parliament has, at least in modern times, accepted that its legislation is stitched or patched into the general fabric of judge-made law. While legislative sovereignty— subject only to the Act of Union with Scotland and sections 2 and 3 of the European Communities Act 1972— belongs, we all know, to Parliament, its statutes are drafted with a limited purpose, which the draftsman formulates in the long title of the Bill and then develops in detail by clauses designed to achieve that purpose. So it is that our statutes are complex and detailed often to the point of unintelligibility and seldom contain any broad declaration of principle. It is consistent with this conception of the character of statute law that the House of Commons will not allow its committees to raise an amendment which goes beyond the scope of a Bill as described in its long title (S.O. 42). Thus, by a self-denying practice which impliedly recognises the existence of the all-pervading customary law, Parliament does not codify. There exist famous statutes which effect, within defined limits, a substitution of statute law for the pre-existing rules of the common law and equity: *e.g.* the Bills of Exchange Act 1882, Sale of Goods Act 1893, Law of Property Act 1925. We also have great statutes which have added new dimensions to the law, creating rights and obligations where before there were none: for instance, the post-war Town and Country Planning legislation beginning with the germinal Act of 1947 and the "welfare" legislation now consolidated into the National Insurance Act and the Social Security Act 1966. But every one of these limited codes is enacted in a scene of which the back-cloth is the customary law, developed by the courts and in which the principal actors are the judges and the legal profession, educated in and loyal to the principles and attitudes of that customary law.

This system of lawyers' law, conceived, developed, and from time to time adjusted by the judges and the legal profession through the forensic process, has had great consequences for the substance and administration of English law. Its shape and content are lawyer-made: its home-made principles, concepts and classifications dominate the education and the thinking of the profession and control legal practice in and out of court. They are preserved and perpetuated by a strict system of precedent which requires inferior courts to follow the law laid down by the Court of Appeal and the House of Lords, and the Court of Appeal to follow the House of Lords and its own previous decisions. The House of Lords does now enjoy—if that be the appropriate word—the freedom not to follow its own previous decisions—a freedom only very recently acquired,[1] and not, it would seem, likely by over-use to degenerate into licence.

The sketch I have drawn sufficiently outlines the overall design of our law to enable the following comments to be made with confidence. The essence of the legal system is that it has been created, developed, and is still

---

[1] July 26, 1966: H.L. Debs. Col. 677.

controlled by the legal profession. It has gone the way the profession, led by the judges, has thought fit, save when Parliament has felt it necessary to make corrections or additions. Though statutes now abound and the statute law is increasing in importance, the legal system is not codified—the background of every statute is the common law—the artifice of the lawyers who, through the medium of the courts, make the rules. The system would not have survived until now, had it not possessed great strengths. First, its independence: created and cherished by the judges, owing nothing in origin to Parliament, claiming to be customary law, it has an in-built resistance to the power of others, whether they be barons or trade unions, Kings or government departments, or even Parliament herself. Its very existence is, therefore, a bulwark against oppression and tyranny, no matter who be the potential oppressor or tyrant. Secondly, it is very professional: developed by the judges and the profession, it is well understood by them, and is handled by them with great self-confidence. This is illustrated by the tradition of oral argument and *ex tempore* judgment in our courts, a process which helps to make the English forensic process one of the swiftest (and least boring) in the world. Thirdly, the system of judicial precedent, made flexible by judicial artistry in " distinguishing cases " and judicial skill in selecting not only the law applicable to the facts of a case, but sometimes the facts as well (*e.g.* the judicial phrase, " the relevant facts "), possesses its own innate balance between certainty and flexibility, the intractable dilemma upon the horns of which every legal system sits—to its own great discomfort. But its weaknesses are also obvious. The law is very much the esoteric business of lawyers. It is neither easily accessible nor easy to understand when found. It is resistant to change: encapsulated in the forensic process, jealously guarded by those tireless workers in the legal hive, the teachers and the practitioners, it can have no greater sensitivity to the winds, let alone the gentle breezes, of change than have the judges and the profession who administer it; and it is no criticism of the legal profession to comment that, faced with the choice between certainty and flexibility, most of them will choose certainty, upholding the established rule, even if it be shown to operate harshly or even unjustly: for their practice and experience will have demonstrated the inestimable value to clients, litigants, and (I would add) students also, of certainty in the law.

In these lectures I can discuss only a few of the current challenges to the system. I have fought off the temptation to discuss the criminal law, largely because its problems and its responses are well-known, being the subject of an enormous literature, lay as well as professional. The challenges I have selected are:

(1) The challenge from overseas—the international movement to secure human rights, and the Common Market.

(2) The social challenge: family life and social security.

(3) The challenge of the environment.

(4) The industrial challenge, and

(5) The regional challenge.

I shall endeavour to measure the extent and implications of each challenge and the law's response, and finally to address myself to the question whether our system can meet them or must be discarded. As I hope to be able to convince you that, granted the will for reform, our system has the principle and the flexibility needed to meet and absorb these challenges, I shall conclude with a passage on the new dimension needed, if the law is to adjust itself to meet its modern challenges.

PART II

THE CHALLENGE FROM OVERSEAS

THE common law has been, like the works of William Shakespeare, one of our most successful exports. The Empire has disappeared: but the common law continues to dominate legal thinking in North America, Australia, New Zealand, and much of Africa: it is also a potent force in the Indian sub-continent. The traffic of the law has not been wholly one-way: wherever the common law has taken root, it has grown, developing new ideas, new approaches to old problems and sending them home. Every academic and practising lawyer has personal knowledge of some of the case law of the United States, Australia, and New Zealand. In many respects the law in these countries has gone further to meet current challenges than the English law: for instance, the United States courts have made progress with the right of privacy and the rights of the unborn child which outdistances anything we in England have yet succeeded in doing.[2]

The success of the common law overseas derives largely from the fact that wherever it went, it found a legal vacuum. Sometimes it was natural as in the empty lands of Australia: sometimes it was artificially created as in India where the British insisted on themselves

---

[2] But we have made a beginning: see the Law Commission's report, Cmnd. 5709 (Law Com. No. 60).

being governed by their own law. And in some lands, as in central Africa and great areas of North America, the existing systems of law were too primitive to compete with the imported product. And so, for one reason or another, the common law when it went overseas seldom had to react to a rival system of developed law: when it did meet such a system, as in Canada and South Africa, it chose to stand aloof, either accepting a territorial limit to its jurisdiction or quietly withdrawing. Thus, despite its world-wide expansion, it learnt surprisingly little from other legal systems. Paradoxically, now that its days of expansion are over, it is more open to foreign influence and challenge than when it strode the world as part of the British colossus: perhaps, in the shadow of that colossus, no other system had a chance.

(a) *The Human Rights Movement*

Amongst the more powerful outside influences to which our legal system is now exposed is that of internationally organised opinion on social and economic as well as political questions. In the twentieth century international affairs are no longer only the business of sovereign states. International law is concerned to protect individual human beings. An early illustration of this concern is in the rules of war.[3] The conduct of war has lost some of its cruelty to individuals since enlightened opinion induced sovereign states to accept the International Convention

---

[3] An excellent short description of the development of the rules of war is to be found in Oppenheim's *International Law*, 6th ed. Vol. II at p. 178 *et seq.*

concerning the laws and custom of war on land (The Hague, 1907). But true progress began with the establishment of the League of Nations after the 1914–1918 war. The League of Nations, and its successor the United Nations Organisation, have done much for individual human beings. The International Labour Organisation, brought into being as part of the League of Nations in 1919, has sought with considerable success to improve standards of safety and health and welfare in industry. The human rights movement is a classical illustration of this beneficent challenge to municipal law. The ILO is entitled to be regarded as a vital first step in the international recognition of human rights: when its objectives were restated in the Declaration of Philadelphia 1946, the organisation was declared to be based on the view that (1) labour is not a mere commercial commodity, (2) freedom of expression and association are essential to progress in industrial affairs, (3) poverty anywhere is a threat not only to prosperity everywhere but to human rights. The Charter of the United Nations (June 26, 1945) declared the determination of the *peoples* (I underline the word) of the United Nations to re-affirm their faith in human rights; and on December 10, 1948, there was adopted by the General Assembly the Universal Declaration of Human Rights.

This great document contains 30 articles preceded by a preamble. Its meaning and intent are clear: it spells out in language all men can understand the human rights that are to be considered " fundamental " and then provides:

By Article 8 that " everyone has the right to an effective remedy by the competent national tribunals for acts violating the fundamental rights granted him by the constitution or by law ";

By Article 28 that " everyone is entitled to a social and international order in which the rights and freedoms set forth in this Declaration can be fully realised ";

And by Article 30 that " nothing in this Declaration may be interpreted as implying for any state group or person any right to engage in any activity or to perform any act aimed at the destruction of any of the rights and freedoms set forth herein." [4]

There can be no doubt as to the message: no person, no institution, no group or body of men may by act or omission diminish the rights declared to be fundamental. The language is apt to include representative and legislative institutions such as Parliament itself as well as more obvious, and more likely, offenders.

In Europe the Declaration was quickly implemented. On November 4, 1950, the Council of Europe adopted the European Convention for the Protection of Human Rights and Fundamental Freedoms.[5] The United Kingdom was the first state to deposit its instrument of ratification. 14 other European states have followed suit: and in some of them ratification means that the provisions of the Convention are already part of their municipal law. It may be that since the passing of the

---

[4] Human Rights, International Instruments of the U.N., New York, 1967.
[5] Conventions and Agreements, Vol. I, p. 22, Strasbourg, 1971.

European Communities Act 1972 the Convention already has, or will, without further enactment by the British Parliament, become part of English law. The Convention includes within its provisions most (though not all) of the human rights declared by the United Nations to be fundamental and creates machinery for their enforcement—a Commission of Human Rights and a Court of Human Rights. Any state which is party to the Convention may refer any alleged breach of the Convention by another party state to the Commission which must consider the complaint, attempt (if it thinks fit) a friendly settlement, and, if the attempt fails, report on the facts and state its opinion. Article 48 makes provision for a reference by the Commission or a party state to the Court.

A significant feature of the Convention is that it affords an opportunity, albeit limited, for an individual person to seek redress. He may make petition, through the Council of Europe, to the Commission, if the party state against whom he petitions has recognised the competence of the Commission to receive such petitions. The United Kingdom did so in 1967 and has renewed its declaration of recognition for a future period. The opportunity is limited, because an individual cannot thereafter take his case to the Court: but, if it be so minded, the Commission can do so for him. By its adherence to these international instruments the United Kingdom has recognised and declared the existence of fundamental human rights, has recognised the right of individuals to have an effective remedy for their violation in the courts of the land, and has accepted the competence of the Commission to consider individuals' complaints of violation, and, at its discretion, to refer any such complaint that it believes to be well-founded to the Court of Human Rights.

Such in outline is the challenge of the Human Rights movement—a movement whose direct legal impact, in so far as it concerns the United Kingdom, has been almost wholly confined to date to the international field.[6] Neither the Declaration of 1948 nor the Convention of 1950 are part of the municipal law of the Kingdom: they can be made so only by Act of Parliament (or, conceivably, by legislative action of the EEC). Yet both instruments reflect a rising tide of opinion which, one way or another, will have to be accommodated in the English legal system. This may be thought to be difficult stuff for the common law. Charters, constitutions, broadly generalised declarations of right, just do not fit. We have no written constitution: our one charter is to be found in a document of 1297 entitled "Magna Carta de Libertatibus Angliae et de Libertatibus Foreste: confirmata a Rege Edwardo,"[7] the key provision of which is often said only to be concerned to ensure that barons are tried by barons: and the one great declaration of human rights conceived and drafted by common lawyers owes its origin to rebellion, and is no part of the law of England. There are many who believe that the response

---

[6] But there are current newspaper reports of the case now before the court of Mr. Golder who alleges he was denied access to his lawyers while in custody in a British prison.

[7] *Halsbury, Statutes*, 3rd ed., Vol. 6, p. 412.

of the common law to pressure for the incorporation of a declaration of human rights into English law should be, quite simply, that it is unnecessary. The point is a fair one and deserves to be taken seriously. When times are normal and fear is not stalking the land, English law sturdily protects the freedom of the individual and respects human personality. But when times are abnormally alive with fear and prejudice, the common law is at a disadvantage: it cannot resist the will, however frightened and prejudiced it may be, of Parliament. The classic illustration is, of course, Regulation 18 (b) and *Liversidge* v. *Anderson* [1942] A.C. 206, when under the pressure of war the judges accepted an interpretation of statutory words which Lord Atkin (page 232) dubbed as " fantastic," and an argument which he thought could have been addressed " acceptably to the Court of King's Bench in the time of Charles I " (page 244). But there are other, and more recent, examples—notably the inability of the courts to correct the retrospective effect of the Immigration Act 1971. It is the helplessness of the law in face of the legislative sovereignty of Parliament which makes it difficult for the legal system to accommodate the concept of fundamental and inviolable human rights. Means therefore have to be found whereby (1) there is incorporated into English law a declaration of such rights, (2) these rights are protected against all encroachment, including the power of the state, even when that power is exerted by a representative legislative institution such as Parliament.

Both these ideas are strange to the present generation

of common lawyers, who have received their legal education against the background of nineteenth century legal thought, which discouraged statutes framed in broad or general terms and acknowledged a complete obedience to the enacted word of Parliament. But it would be wrong, I submit, to assume that the nineteenth century view of the common law (which owes much to Bentham who disliked Declarations of Rights and to Austin who accepted as inevitable the unrestricted legislative sovereignty of Parliament) is necessarily correct or complete. In a most revealing chapter in his book on Human Rights [8] Professor Lauterpacht has drawn attention to some features in the development of the common law which nineteenth-century thinkers chose to disregard. He mentions " the English constitutional practice of safeguarding the rights of the subject by statutory enactment," *e.g.* Magna Carta, Habeas Corpus, the Bill of Rights and the Act of Settlement. And he challenges the proposition that " the very conception of inalienable and fundamental rights superior to the State was unknown to English legal and political tradition." In other words he challenges the view that, by common law, our rights were secured by the courts only against the Executive, and not against the Legislature. Historically the question is wide open. As Sir Frederick Pollock has remarked,[9] " The omnipotence of Parliament was not the orthodox theory of English law, if orthodox at all, in Holt's time."

---

[8] *International Law and Human Rights* (London, 1950), Chap. 8 (more particularly, pp. 128 and 134).

[9] 39 L.Q.R. 165.

Sir Edward Coke was never easy in his mind when Parliament's unrestricted supremacy was urged upon him: for example, *Doctor Bonham's* case [10]; and in *Foster's* case he declared that the words of an Act of Parliament "shall not bind the King's Bench because the pleas there are *coram ipso Rege*." [11] Professor Lauterpacht also calls attention (page 128) to a quotation from Oliver Cromwell, which deserves to be remembered in the twentieth century: "In every Government there must be Somewhat Fundamental, Somewhat like a Magna Charter, which should be standing, be unalterable,... That Parliaments should not make themselves perpetual is a Fundamental. Of what assurance is a law to prevent so great an evil, if it lie in the same legislature to un-law it again." With such views prevalent in the seventeenth century it need cause no wonder that, when in the eighteenth century the American colonists drafted their various declarations of rights, they saw nothing strange in seeking by legal process to curb the legislative sovereignty of Parliament: nor, when they achieved independence and wrote their own constitution, did they feel it in any way anomalous to control the power of the legislature as well as that of the executive. While, therefore, we must recognise that English law does today accept as beyond legal challenge the legislative sovereignty of Parliament, there is nothing in its tradition or heritage that makes such acceptance so basic that, if it be limited, the system would collapse. On the contrary,

---

[10] (1615) 11 Co.Rep. 565, at p. 645.
[11] Coke C.J. in *Foster's* case, 11 Co.Rep. 1222, at p. 1234.

history and the American experience both suggest that adjustment can be made, if it be thought desirable. And I submit that it is desirable—perhaps even inevitable, if the United Kingdom is fully to honour its international obligations, and if its law is to meet the demands of a rising public opinion. Two courses are, I think, open: one for the law to pursue its present inclination to ignore the Human Rights movement, making the assumption that the existing English law is a substantial compliance with our international obligations; the other, to give thought to a new constitutional settlement whereby it would be made very much more difficult to repeal certain statutes than others—that is to say, the acceptance of entrenched provisions as part of our statute law. The first course is, I submit, one we should reject. So long as English law is unable in any circumstances to challenge a statute, it is, in dangerous and difficult times, at the mercy of the oppressive and discriminatory statute. Secondly, even when times are such that Parliament does not feel the need for so-called emergency legislation, the absence of entrenched provisions protecting human rights can have unacceptable consequences. Do you think that the deeply disturbing practices of interrogation to which resort was had in Northern Ireland would have occurred, had British law possessed at the time a fully developed code of fundamental human rights? And, if despite the existence of such a code men had been subjected to the oppressive and degrading interrogation techniques described in the Compton Report,[12] would the

---

[12] August 9, 1971 (Cmnd. 4823).

United Kingdom now be standing at the bar of European justice, trying to explain that, though our law says nothing, yet it does provide a sufficient remedy? Put at its mildest, the present situation of the United Kingdom at the bar of European justice and in the eyes of international legal opinion is embarrassing—defendants at the suit of the Republic of Ireland alleging the torture of prisoners; and, in another matter, we are about to become defendants to a petition by a London newspaper alleging that English law, as authoritatively declared by the House of Lords, in the recent " contempt of court " proceedings arising out of the thalidomide tragedy, failed to protect adequately the right of freedom of speech.

One does not know what the outcome of the pending proceedings in Strasbourg will be. But they illustrate a challenge the law must face if it is to continue to be acceptable. They expose an unresolved difference between our legal system and our international obligations. If the difference be not resolved, we shall be faced, sooner or later, with an international finding that English law fails to provide a remedy which the United Kingdom is bound by international law to provide. A legal system of which that can be said is a legal system under threat: and the common law to survive will have to find its answer. I see no reason why the answer should not be a new constitutional settlement. It is no longer enough to say, with Magna Carta, " no free man shall be taken or imprisoned ... or any otherwise destroyed, nor will we pass upon him nor deal with him but by lawful judgment of his peers, or by the law of the land." The legal system must now ensure that the law of the land will itself meet the exacting standards of human rights declared by international instruments, to which the United Kingdom is a party, as inviolable. This calls for entrenched or fundamental laws protected by a Bill of Rights—a constitutional law which it is the duty of the courts to protect even against the power of Parliament. In other words, there must be a constitutional restraint placed upon the legislative power which is designed to protect the individual citizen from instant legislation, conceived in fear or prejudice and enacted in breach of human rights.

Though such is not yet the constitutional position in England, I have sought to give you the reasons why I see no difficulty of principle in the common law adjusting itself successfully to a written constitution and entrenched provisions. Both the United States and the Republic of Ireland have enacted constitutional guarantees for the rights of individual citizens without peril to the common law which their courts administer. Before the era of untrammelled legislative sovereignty imposed upon the modern law by Parliament's victory in the seventeenth century and made respectable by the theories of Bentham and Austin in the nineteenth, the common law judges felt able to sit in judgment upon a statute and our legislators did not shrink from enactments that were intended to play the part of entrenched provisions protecting the fundamental rights of the individual— Magna Carta, Habeas Corpus for instance. There is no reason why the common law should not accept a return to earlier attitudes: no reason why a curb should not be placed on Parliament herself when the issue is one of human rights.

(b) *The Common Market*

When in 1950 Professor Lauterpacht remarked that " it is not inconceivable that the supremacy of Parliament may be deliberately made to yield to an International Bill of Rights," he was speaking of human rights. But his words were prophetic: the process of yielding to an international instrument has begun with sections 2 and 3 of the European Communities Act 1972 which acknowledges the existence of a source of law and a court uncontrolled by Parliament. The Common Market is the second of the international challenges I propose to consider. The law of the European Communities derives from three treaties: the Treaty of Rome establishing the Economic Community, the Treaty of Paris establishing the Coal and Steel Community, and the Euratom Treaty establishing the Atomic Community. The three communities share one set of institutions: a Council of Ministers, the European Commission, the European Court of Justice, and an Assembly (misleadingly called the European Parliament: it has, as yet, no electorate and precious little power). The Treaties, or part of them are now English law giving rise to rights and obligations enforceable in our courts: section 2 (1) of the Act of 1972 introduces into the law what it calls " enforceable community right," an expression which covers any right, power, liability or obligation arising under the Treaties which the Treaties require to be given legal effect in the

United Kingdom. This provision introduces into the law far more than merely the Treaties themselves, bulky though they are: for each Treaty (I shall henceforth, for the sake of simplicity, refer only to the Treaty of Rome since it may be regarded as typical of all three) confers upon the Council of Ministers and the European Commission law-making powers. Article 189 of the Treaty places upon the Council and the Commission the duty to " make regulations, issue directives, take decisions." The article goes on to provide: " A regulation shall apply generally. It shall be binding in its entirety and take direct effect in each member state. A directive shall be binding, as to the result to be achieved, upon each member state to which it is directed, while leaving to national authorities the choice of form and method. A decision shall be binding in its entirety upon those to whom it is directed." Section 3 (1) of the European Communities Act provides that any question as to the meaning and effect of the Treaties and their subordinate legislation is a question of law to be determined, in the ultimate resort, by the European Court. No need for me to emphasise that there is here a potent new source of English law. Its volume is already considerable, though its impact has not yet been widely felt. Our legal system has, therefore, to adjust itself to a new-style statute law, the drafting and ultimate interpretation of which are the responsibility of institutions other than the Parliament and courts of the Kingdom. The powers of the European court are considerable: and the indications are that it is determined to use them. The duty of the court is to

" ensure that the law is observed in the interpretation and implementation " of the Treaty (article 164). Both the Commission (article 169) and any member state can bring before the court a member state alleged to have infringed any of its Treaty obligations. But in considering the challenge to our legal system of this new law, the important provisions are those which concern private individuals. The court (its filial relationship to the French Conseil d'Etat is very obvious to those who know the parent) has the duty of supervising the legality of measures taken by the Council and the Commission and jurisdiction to quash any measure which is shown to have been *ultra vires* or to constitute an infringement " of important procedural rules ... of this Treaty or of any rule of law relating to its application, or misuse of powers." This jurisdiction to quash can be invoked by " any natural or legal person " if the decision be of direct and individual concern to him—as well, of course, as by the Council, Commission or a member state. Further, it would appear that the aggrieved citizen, should he succeed, would be able to obtain monetary compensation as well as a quashing of the illegal measure: see articles 176 and 215. The power of the court to determine the true meaning and effect of the Treaty and the subordinate legislation deriving from it (*e.g.* regulations, directives, decisions) is conferred by article 177 which provides for reference of any such question from the national courts to the European court. Reference is at the discretion of the national court save that, where such a question is raised in a court from which there is no possibility of appeal under the national law, reference is compulsory.

Finally, the decisions of the European institutions are given teeth. Article 192 provides that a decision of the Council or Commission which involves a pecuniary obligation upon a person other than a State shall be enforceable by the ordinary processes for the execution of civil judgments and that enforcement may be suspended only by a decision of the European court.

There are Plantagenet echoes about this new legal world. The citizen has little say in the preparation of its legislation: his own representative Parliament will find it difficult, if not impossible, to make its voice effectively heard in the process of legislation and the European Assembly possesses only one power, that of sacking the Commission—which might be thought to be, in Plantagenet idiom, akin to the power to refuse the King money, and, in modern idiom, to the use of a nuclear weapon to control a street riot. But, as in Plantagenet times, the citizen does have recourse to the courts: and until such time as the legislative process of the Communities is improved, this recourse is the one effective safeguard of his rights and liberties in the field covered by the law of the Communities. His recourse, as I have described, is twofold, though the ultimate arbiter in each case is the European court. If he takes his grievance direct to that court, English law is only marginally concerned—to the extent that his action may lead to the quashing of a measure which would otherwise have legal effect in this country. But, if a question arises in English litigation as to the meaning, effect, or validity of a Community measure, the English court has to decide it in accordance with the principles laid down by, and any relevant decision of, the European court. In such a situation the English court has to grapple with new-style statute law, and new-style principles of interpretation derived from the codified systems of Europe, and has to accept, upon reference, the ruling of a new-style court whose approach to its task has the strong activist element that one finds in the French Conseil d'Etat.

It is too early yet to gauge the impact of all this upon our law.[13] The Court of Appeal has begun its study of the problem: the House of Lords has yet to face it. In *Bulmer Limited and Anor.* v. *Bollinger S.A. and Anor.*,[14] Lord Denning examined the impact of the new law and the new court upon English law. To quote his dazzling simile, " The Treaty is like an incoming tide. It flows into the estuaries and up the rivers. It cannot be held back." And later he said: " We must no longer speak or think of English law as something on its own. We must speak and think of Community law, of Community rights and obligations, and we must give effect to them. This means a great effort for the lawyers. We have to learn a new system." He went on to demonstrate that the new system was based on statutes differently drafted—more general, less detailed and complex than the English model; on principles of interpretation which accord to

---

[13] September 1974.
[14] [1974] 3 W.L.R. 202; 118 S.J. 404; [1974] 2 All E.R. 1226; [1974] F.S.R. 334; [1974] 2 C.M.L.R. 91, C.A.

the courts the positive role of ensuring that the policy and intent of the statute are not defeated by obscurities, ambiguities or omissions in its wording, a role which includes the power of bridging gaps by " judicial legislation " (goodbye to Lord Simonds and *Magor R.D.C.* v. *Newport U.D.C.*): and on a Continental approach to existing case law which treats it as never more than persuasive—though it can be very persuasive—but as always capable of being departed from, if the circumstances of the Community as understood by the European Court require it. For the moment, to adopt Lord Denning's imagery, the incoming tide has not yet mingled with the home waters of the common law: but it is inconceivable that, like the Rhone and the Arve where those two streams meet at Geneva, they should move on, side by side, one grey with the melted snows and ice of the distant mountains of our legal history, the other blue and clear, reflecting modern opinion. If we stay in the Common Market, I would expect to see its principles of legislation and statutory interpretation and its conception of an activist court whose role is to strengthen and fulfil the purpose of statute law replace the traditional attitudes of English judges and lawyers to statute law and the current complex style of statutory drafting. The trend away from a system, in which customary law is the general rule, and statute the exception, was already a significant one before our entry into the Common Market, though the old theory still dominates legal education and thinking. Community law could well mean that the theory of a common law (and equity) locked in the breasts of the judges and helped out, when necessary, by Acts of Parliament will soon be of interest only to legal historians.

To sum up the international challenge, it poses, I submit, some fundamental questions. The legislative sovereignty of Parliament and the existence of a common or customary law, where statute is silent, are, both of them, under challenge. The power of Parliament to make what law it likes and the power of the judges, using a strict doctrine of judicial precedent, to declare what the law is in those areas untouched by statute would seem to be contrary to the international obligations accepted by the United Kingdom. A new constitutional settlement may well be needed which establishes not only a new relationship between enacted and judge-made law, but a new breed of enacted law in which there is a distinction drawn between fundamental and other laws, the former not to be overthrown merely at the will of a bare parliamentary majority. The " command " theory which has lain in the roots of our statute law for so long may have to yield to a *jus gentium* arising outside Parliament, interpreted in the last resort by an international court, but enforced by our courts as part and parcel of our municipal law.

PART III

THE SOCIAL CHALLENGE

THE challenge from overseas has shown the common law in modern dress at a disadvantage in two respects. First, arraigned at the bar of international opinion, it has to admit to a weakness in its protection of human rights: it is powerless when confronted with the legislative sovereignty of Parliament.

Secondly, it is now faced by the EEC with a codified law, already part and parcel of English law, which is drafted in a way wholly strange to English legal practice and is interpreted by an activist, French-style court which has both the duty to ensure that the code is effectively implemented and the power to restrain the legislative as well as the executive organs of the Community from acting outside the code. But there are other challenges besides the international one: and, in particular, the social challenge, to which I now come.

The social challenge arises from a combination of two recently emerged but fundamental social beliefs. The first is that men, and women, are not to be denied the opportunities of personal happiness, to be achieved not as others think fit, but as they wish it. The second is that we are all entitled to the active protection of the state against the ills of poverty, disease and old age. The fair distribution of wealth among all members of society has become a human right as important to the law as the right of property.

This social change is currently a most formidable threat to the English legal system, as we know it today. Social justice, by which today's society means justice in depth not only penetrating and destroying the inequalities of sex, race and wealth but also supporting the weak and the exposed, is believed by some to be beyond the reach of the traditional combination of common law rule and equitable relief supplemented where necessary, by statute: it appears to need new law, new principles, new remedies, new machinery and new men.[15]

Undoubtedly a more positive approach is now called for from the law to the problems of daily life, if only because a more positive contribution in terms of money and administrative help is called for from the government. It is no longer sufficient for the law to provide a framework of freedom in which men, women and children may work out their own destinies: social justice, as our society now understands the term, requires the law to be loaded in favour of the weak and the exposed, to provide them with financial and other support, and with access to courts, tribunals, and other administrative agencies where their rights can be enforced.

The demand for new law makes its impact in those fields more particularly concerned with the weak and the exposed, notably in the fields of health, housing, national

---

[15] For example, Titmuss, who doubted whether lawyers have any contribution to make to the work of the social security system: 1971, *Political Quarterly*, Vol. 42, p. 113.

insurance, supplementary benefit, race relations and immigration—in all of which one finds significantly the role of the traditional courts and the legal profession questioned in theory and diminished in practice, and responsibility placed upon new-style decision-making bodies, some of which (*e.g.* the Supplementary Benefit Appeals Tribunals) have only the most tenuous link with the legal system.

I propose to consider in any detail only one aspect of the challenge—its impact upon the law relating to family life—but the existence of the total challenge must not be overlooked; it is an integral part of my argument. English family law is of recent origin: until the mid-nineteenth century, family life was not the law's concern, but the business of the church. So long as a man avoided criminal violence towards, or criminal neglect of, his wife and children, it was felt that the law should not intervene unless there was some property interest to protect. A few great nineteenth-century statutes transformed the picture bringing the secular law into family life. In 1857 the Matrimonial Causes Act transferred jurisdiction over broken marriages from the ecclesiastical courts to a secular court, the " Court for Divorce and Matrimonial Causes " and conferred upon the new court the power to dissolve a marriage. The new principle of judicial divorce, thus introduced, was that a broken marriage could be treated like any other civil wrong; prove the wrong done to you, and the law will grant its remedy. The new law achieved more for men by offering them—at a price— judicial divorce from an adulteress wife than for women, who could obtain a divorce only if they could show adultery was accompanied by some other offence such as cruelty or desertion. But, though it accepted the inequality of women before the law, it offered them, too, a remedy, where previously there had been none.

Contemporaneously with the liberalisation of the divorce laws [16] Parliament concerned itself with securing to married women their separate property [17] and, more significantly, with extending some measure of matrimonial relief to those too poor to afford the release of divorce.

In 1878 magistrates, sitting in the courts of summary jurisdiction, were given jurisdiction by section 4 of the Matrimonial Causes Act, of *that year*, to order a husband, convicted of aggravated assault upon his wife, to pay money for her support, if they were satisfied that her future safety required the making of a non-cohabitation order.[18]

From this section developed the extensive jurisdiction of the magistrates' court in matrimonial affairs—for nearly 100 years the poor man's and poor woman's substitute for divorce which remained a remedy that neither he nor she could afford despite the reforms. The later Victorians were also deeply troubled at the fate of the children of broken homes. The same section empowered

---

[16] Vigorously opposed by Gladstone: even the " liberal " establishment has always found divorce reform hard to swallow: see " Gladstone," *Magnus* (London, 1954), pp. 130–131.

[17] The culminating statute was the Married Women's Property Act 1882 which consolidated and amended the earlier Acts.

[18] 41 & 42 Vict. c. 19.

the magistrates to give the custody of the children to the wife, and in 1886 the Guardianship of Infants Act provided that, wherever a court was concerned with the custody or upbringing of a child, it must treat the child's welfare as the first and paramount consideration.

Thus by the end of the nineteenth century the ordinary courts of the land had been given the job of dealing with broken marriages; divorce, judicial separation, nullity, maintenance, property, and the custody of children were for them, acting under a law based on the matrimonial offence but recognising the primacy of the children's welfare.

The twentieth century has seen fundamental changes in this law. The principle of the matrimonial offence came under pressure, and is now destroyed. In 1937 A. P. Herbert's Act introduced into the law a ground of divorce without guilt, namely, incurable insanity of five years' duration; at last, in 1969, Parliament put an end to a divorce law which had come to be disregarded in practice—by the Divorce Reform Act eliminating the doctrine of the matrimonial offence: there is now only one ground of divorce, irretrievable breakdown of marriage.[19] The inequality of women in the family has been eliminated, though it was not until 1973 that a

---

[19] These quiet achievements have taken time. The climacteric steps were: the Gorell Report (1912) Cd. 6478–6482, the Matrimonial Causes Act 1937, "Putting Asunder": S.P.C.K. 1966, "Field of Choice," Law Com. No. 6 and the Divorce Reform Act 1969. None of this would have been achieved without the dedicated work of backbench members of Parliament. The establishment, with the notable exception of Lord Chancellor Gardiner, held aloof.

statute [20] declared her rights as a parent to be precisely the same as those of the father. Further, the courts have been strengthened when dealing with children's problems by the institution in 1950 and the ensuing development of the office of the Court Welfare Officer.[21] Lastly—the most valuable, in practice, of the reforms—the courts have been made accessible to all by the provision of free legal aid and advice to those who cannot afford it.[22]

The point I wish to make about these developments is that they have been effected within the framework of the existing legal system.

In other words, the system of the common law with its emphasis upon judge-made law and its conception of the importance of the adversary-type trial was extended to embrace the problems of the broken marriage. In this way the canon law of the church, administered by the ecclesiastical courts, was replaced by a family law transferred to the established legal system and based on the concepts of the common law.

And so it has happened that the development of the family law posed, until recently, no real threat to the established law: it had proved to be a reform which could be effectuated without any wrench to the system. The achievement is a memorable illustration of the flexibility of our law, its ability to accommodate, when it cannot resist, change.

---

[20] The Guardianship Act 1973.
[21] For a short account of its beginnings, see King, *The Probation Service* (London, 1964), p. 41.
[22] Legal Aid and Advice Act 1949: the existing law is now to be found in the consolidating statute, Legal Aid Act 1974.

This flexibility is part of the secret of our law's survival. English law, it can be said, throughout its history has imitated the feat of the late, and very long-lived, Lady Mendel, who was always able to stand on her head, and frequently did so: or, to take another comparable, it has much in common with the Vicar of Bray.

The lady, the parson and the law have lived long. Though it be a digression, a short reference to two of the somersaults of English law can illustrate the superb flexibility of its muscles. It conserved and regulated the feudal system for centuries: but when the divine right of kings, feudal tenure and the burden of feudal services were laid to rest finally in the seventeenth century, the law adjusted itself without any sign of stress to the principles of the freedom of man—limited only by the need to preserve society—a philosophy of which Locke was the finest English exponent.

When freedom was found to leave the problems of the weak and the socially exploited unsolved, the law changed direction under the guidance of thinkers such as Jeremy Bentham and John Stuart Mill. Then came the changes in the substantive law, *e.g.* the nineteenth-century development of the rights of men, women and children in the fields of employment, property, and family life.

But now more is seen to be required; the state has become a welcome intruder into the social life of the community with its money and its administration, erecting the social security system as an integral part of the welfare state. The management and control of the social security system represent one of the great modern challenges to the law's flexibility in the pursuit of survival. On this aspect of the social challenge the law's response has been, so far, hesitant and confused. There are two basic problems: is it desirable that the social security system should be subjected to " the legal treatment "— *i.e.* advice, assistance, and control? If it is, has the legal system, as we know it, the flexibility to meet the challenge? There is the strong possibility of a qualified answer to the first question, which would then raise the consequential question: to what extent should the social security system be tied into the general legal system?

First the facts. The truth is that the system of social security is so far removed from the practice of the law that very few lawyers have any but the haziest idea of its nature and content. Ignorance of the field to be covered is a poor beginning for the establishment there of the rule of law: but this is where we begin.

There are no text books, though I am glad to see some are now promised.[23] The material for study—apart from the legislation itself—consists of pamphlets (even booklets) issued by government agencies, notably the DHSS (and its predecessors), a few admirable paperback publications [24] written to help a puzzled public, and a growing research literature so esoteric in character as to be of

---

[23] September 1974, The Citizens' Advice Notes (CANS), published by the National Council of Social Services, is a mine of information.
[24] Phyllis Willmott, *Consumers' Guide to the British Social Services*, Pelican, 3rd ed. 1973; Tony Lynes, *The Penguin Guide to Supplementary Benefits*, 1972; Anna Coote and Tess Gill, *Women's Rights : A Practical Guide*, Penguin, 1974.

little use to the citizen in need. On a recent count the author of one paperback found some 76 " commonly needed pamphlets and leaflets " available free at government offices.[25] The Stationery Office has published an admirable handbook on Supplementary Benefits: but the benefit is administered according to an unpublished code " which [to quote the S.B.C.] is largely unintelligible to the lay reader and which, therefore, the commission has decided [is] unsuitable for publication." [26] This is a mercy, no doubt, for most of us: but the implications of the decision are ominous. Equally obscure is the learning about national insurance, though there exists in this branch of the system a more highly developed legal control than elsewhere and, therefore, some case law. Yet, to quote from Anna Coote's and Tessa Gill's sparkling guide to women's rights:

> " The National Insurance Scheme is a bureaucrat's dream. It is so complicated that no one really knows why they are paying money into it each week, what they are getting in return, or what they might be missing if they don't pay. Do you? " [27]

Their question is directed to women. I put it to lawyers and judges: and I suspect I know what would be the truthful answer from the great majority.

The suspicion becomes a probability when I turn to Table I of Phyllis Wilmott's book, which lists " Types

---

[25] Willmott, *op. cit.*
[26] HMSO, 1971. I am indebted for this quotation to Richard White's excellent essay in *Social Needs and Legal Action*, Martin Robertson, 1973.
[27] Coote and Gill, *op. cit.*, p. 65.

of adviser ": she enumerates 34, not one of them a lawyer.

Thus, whatever the theoretical position, the practicality is—an almost total divorce between the law, as administered and practised by lawyers, and the social security system. This may be a good or a bad thing—a question to which I shall return: but, whichever answer you choose to give, the social significance of the *de facto* divorce is very great since the social security system is not only complex but pervasive: it enters into the life of everyone, and is a major factor in the lives of millions.

The first feature of our social security to be noted is that it is not one system but a series of interlocking systems. They include the basic flat-rate scheme of national insurance, the industrial injuries scheme, the various and ever-changing earnings-related pension (and other benefits) schemes which latch on to the basic national insurance scheme, the supplementary benefits scheme (the modern representative of the ancient poor law, but now centrally organised and financed with a uniform scale of a large number of benefits adapted to the manifold needs of the poor and based firmly upon right, not charity), and a number of specific family schemes, *e.g.* family allowances, family income supplement, attendance allowance, and pensions for the over-80s.

The second feature, to which I have already alluded by way of comment on supplementary benefit, is that all the schemes, though decision in particular cases often depends upon exercise of discretion, are based upon entitlement, *i.e.* right. The conditions of entitlement are often very difficult to comprehend even for the trained and experienced mind: the confusion that is likely to overwhelm the mind of the worried, the tense, the impoverished, the sick, the neglected, the unemployed, the injured, and the aged for whom they are intended needs no emphasising. I will give one illustration. The basic national insurance scheme offers a range of nine benefits: in addition, there are available the benefits of the industrial injuries scheme to those who are in insurable employment. The right to the national insurance benefits depends upon a person's contribution record. If you fail to pay all or a stated number of contributions over a defined period, your benefits are at risk: they may be reduced or even become nil. Your contributions include a fraction allocated to the industrial injuries scheme: but benefits under this scheme depend not on payment of contributions but on the existence of insurable employment. The difficulties a claimant may have to face are obvious. How many contributions have been paid? Think of a wife, more especially a separated wife, faced with proving the number of her husband's contributions when she has reason to think the office has got it wrong. Or how many credited? For in certain circumstances payment is not required. Is or was he or she a class 1, a class 2 or a class 3, contributor?: the benefits vary according to the class of the contributions: class 1 being in respect of persons in employment; class 2, the self-employed; and the class 3 those who are not in employment. The administrator says that all the information is in his records and the distinctions clear and fully explained in his literature. But records are sometimes defective: and why should entitlement necessarily be as the administrator interprets it? The citizen may have other ideas; and he may be right.

This brings me to the third feature—the right of appeal from the decision of the appointed government officer or agent. Each scheme has its own made-to-measure, specialised system of administrative tribunals.

The world of the administrative tribunal is invigilated by that watchdog, the Council on Tribunals, set up by the Tribunals and Inquiries Act 1958, which, following the report of the Franks Committee, sought to introduce an element of legal control. The Council's two achievements to date have been the penetration of ideas of natural justice into the procedure of tribunals, and its success in influencing government to appoint legally-trained chairmen to very many tribunals. The size of the world over which it watches is seldom fully grasped by the public. In appendix C to the Council's Report for 1972–73 there are listed as under its general supervision 52 categories of tribunal before whom in the period covered by the report there came over 1 million cases. Of these (I exclude tribunals concerned with tax, rates, rent, road traffic and other areas of activity of critical importance to society, because they are not directly within the context I have set myself) just under 100,000 were cases concerned with social security. Within that figure, supplementary benefit (33,735 appeals), national insurance (32,437) and industrial injuries (18,124) accounted for the bulk of the cases.

I have indicated that thanks to the work of the Council, the procedure of the administrative tribunal has to conform to the rules of natural justice, and that there is a goodly number of legally qualified chairmen. But the distance between this world and the legal system remains. The justice of the decision, as distinct from the legality of their proceedings, is beyond review by the courts: and the legal profession does not, as a general rule, conduct or advise upon cases. There is no embargo on their doing so: but, to quote The Law Society's Report on Legal Aid and Advice for the year 1972–73, the value of the legal aid scheme is grievously hampered by not being available in administrative tribunals. Further, in some tribunals, notably some Supplementary Benefit Appeal tribunals, there is an element of lawyer-resistance: his legalism—the lawyer's endemic disease—is seen as a threat to the system.

Such is the outline, admittedly only sketched, of the social security system operated within the welfare state— the provision of financial and administrative support by the government for all who need it, whatever the reason. The challenge to the law is subtle but pervasive; and unanswerable unless the legal profession is prepared, when it enters this new world, to discard some professional attitudes and practices which, because they have been with us for so long, appear to be fundamental principles of the law.

There is, I think, a group of traditional lawyer's attitudes which create the difficulty. First, the common law is treated as a private law system, concerned essentially with the person, the property, and the reputation of the individual. Its primary concern has been to defend private property and to distribute justice between individuals in disputes with each other. The key figure is the client, seen as one whose property or person has been wrongfully damaged, diminished, or put at risk by another: and the key concept is the cause of action, *i.e.* loss or injury arising or threatened from an infringement of a personal or property right. The business of the courts has thus been distributive justice handed down by the King's judges from their lofty but completely detached position: the state's interest has been to do justice between man and man. Secondly, from this outlook and approach there has arisen the common law's lack of concern with public law—a term so unknown to English lawyers that I feel I must explain myself. Public law is concerned with the rights and obligations of the state in the setting of municipal law. The common law recognises within that setting and subject only to a few unavoidable exceptions no distinction between the servants of the Crown and private persons: the law is the same for the private and for the public sector.

Thirdly, being a " lawyer's law " system based on judicial precedent, it encourages the belief that only lawyers may explain, interpret, and develop it. Although decision in particular cases is frequently left to laymen, it occurs under strict legal guidance: a jury has to take the law from the presiding judge, and the freedom of lay magistrates to determine what the law in a given case is proves on examination to be more apparent than real: the influence of their clerk, and the surveillance of the Divisional Court of the Queen's Bench and Family Divisions of the High Court ensure a very strict control.

These attitudes and practices have nothing in common with the thinking that lies at the root of social security or, more broadly, the welfare state. In this field there is a minimum of private property, and often none: that is why the system exists. There is, basically, only need—need for money, for a home, for medical care, for education, for support: the origin of these needs is an irrelevance, the fact that they exist is what matters. There is no wrongdoer, no adversary: no plaintiff or defendant. And the position of the state is fundamentally changed. It now provides the money and the administration to meet the need. The money and the administrative support are, if eligibility is established, a right possessed by the citizen, an obligation owed to him by the state. Thus at the very heart of the system lies the seed of conflict between the state which owes a duty and the citizen to whom it is owed: the state has descended from the lofty perch of detachment, which is its resting-place in the common law, and is now a participator in an activity which may lead to conflict and require it ultimately to act as judge in a cause in which it has an interest. Finally, the principles which govern social security are not legal rules but policy governing the administration of benefit provided by the state from public funds. The administrator claims, with reason, that he is likely to understand, explain, interpret, and apply policy more effectively and relevantly than lawyers—be they judges or practitioners.

If, therefore, the law and the lawyer are to make a socially valuable contribution to the operation of the social security system, there must be abandoned old-established habits of thought as to the nature of law and the whole gamut of practices summed up in the layman's word of deadly insult, " legalism "—his word for rigid attachment to legal precedent, the substitution of legal rule for policy, the fettering of discretion, the adversary style, the taking of technical points, formality. In their place, we have to accommodate in the legal system a public law which, while it supports the citizen's rights and regulates the actions of the state in conflict situations arising between it and the citizen where the state is the provider, the policy-maker, and the judge, does not destroy the essentially administrative nature of the state's function or overlay policy and discretion with so-called legal rules.

On any view of the problem, this is a large lump for the legal system to digest. Is it necessary to try?

I return now to the question: is it desirable that the social security system should be subjected to " the legal treatment "—advice, assistance, and control?

The system is conceived, undoubtedly, as a system of rights dependent upon eligibility. It contains the possibility of conflict between citizen and state: and in any conflict the citizen may find himself without the physical or material resources, the expertise or knowledge to make his case against the government expert, who, perfectly bona fide but mistakenly, may act in a given case upon the view that the citizen has no entitlement.

These considerations point to the desirability of legal control, and legal advice and assistance; but there are counter-arguments. " Legalism " is seen as a deterrent to many citizens and as a danger to sound administration. Formality may inhibit the citizen; precedent may overlay and even destroy the administrative purpose of the benefit in issue: and the adversary process may displace one in which the aim is that all concerned should be working together as a team to discover the appropriate action required in a given case to satisfy the administrative purpose of the scheme concerned.

Considerable research is being undertaken at present in the hope that an answer may be given to the question of the desirability of " legal treatment." But the broad facts are known. The indications are, as the Lord Chancellor's Advisory Committee on Legal Aid has said in its latest report, that:

" (a) there are many people whose legal rights are, for a variety of reasons, at present going by default, ... [and]

(d) there are considerable areas of the law, notably those relating to housing, landlord and tenant matters and welfare benefits, where expert advice and assistance is, [sic] urgently needed." [28]

I suggest, therefore, that we do not have to wait on research to be able to give a qualified answer. The

---

[28] Law Society and Lord Chancellor's Advisory Committee on Legal Aid and Advice, 23rd Report, 1972/3.

participation of the legal profession in advising and assisting the citizen is desirable to meet the difficulties the citizen experiences in the securing of his rights; but it would be undesirable if lawyers should seek to mould the system to their traditional patterns of litigation and case law. It does not, however, follow that because lawyers' participation in the work of the tribunals is desirable, legal control must also be desirable. Is there, then, a case for greater legal control than can be achieved merely by the appointment of legally qualified chairmen and the adoption of just procedural rules? The question opens up wide questions of the acceptable degree of judicial intervention in the business of administration— *i.e.* the problem of public law in a common law setting.

For myself, I believe that one cannot answer this question until one sees what the legal system has to offer. As I have already mentioned, there is inevitably a conflict situation in the administration of social security; there is, therefore, a requirement for the rule of law in resolving the conflict so that justice can be done—and be seen to be done. On analysis, the conflict is revealed as arising between participants with wholly different objectives— the administrator anxious to husband public funds so that they are expended within the limits of a policy con- ceived and administered by government, and the citizen, who wants his rights. Thus the administrator has an administrative purpose, the citizen a legal objective. The analysis, taken only thus far, is enough to show that an attempt should be made to inject a degree of legal control—*i.e.* review by the ordinary courts which the public recognises as independent and detached from the administration of the benefit in issue. But such a view will offer no comfort to the citizen, unless the courts have the power, albeit strictly defined, to give effect to the merits of a citizen's case. For, were such a powerful and wide-ranging apparatus allowed to operate extra-legally, sooner or later abuse of power, too often accompanied by citizen frustration, would develop—it might even become a habit. Lord Acton's famous aphorism applies to institutions as well as persons: and it would be a disturbing irony if in family life we were to substitute for the common law powers of the husband and father a *patria potestas* in the agencies of the state as uncontrolled as that of the Roman father—but without the natural restraint of fatherly love or family pride.

Though the law must discard some of its historical accretions in meeting the challenge of the welfare state, it does not lack resources for the task. The legal system has a collection of remedies which could be developed to do the job. Since 1947 [29] there has been no procedural obstacle to the law protecting the individual who has suffered loss from the Crown's breach of contract or civil wrong. In addition to the subjection of the Crown to the common law of contract and tort, the law offers certain specialised remedies, the orders of mandamus, prohibition and certiorari, and relief by way of declaration. Mandamus, prohibition, and certiorari are, strictly, not remedies against the Crown—they are orders issued

---

[29] Crown Proceedings Act 1947 (1947, c. 44).

by the King's judges to ensure that inferior tribunals established by the state and the servants of the Crown do what they are required by law to do—no more and no less. Mandamus compels an inferior court or a public officer to do his duty: prohibition and certiorari enable the King's judges to review and keep within the limits of the law the work of inferior courts or tribunals. Their importance, together with that of the Divisional Court of the Queen's Bench Division which administers this branch of the law, has increased greatly with the advent of the administrative tribunal: they do provide the law with its opportunity for controlling the instrument chosen by government for doing justice in the welfare state.

These orders derive from the prerogative writs, similarly named, which they have superseded. The declaratory order is, however, a modern creation. No such remedy was known to the common law in the days when that system was wholly distinct from equity: and in the Court of Chancery a binding declaration could be made only if some right to relief, other than a mere declaration, could be established. But in 1883 a new rule of court introduced what a great judge described as " an innovation of a very important kind," *i.e.* the power of the court to make binding declarations of right, whether or not any consequential relief was or could be claimed.[30] The existence of this power, though it be discretionary (as is also the power to issue the prerogative orders) and sparingly used, is a strong point in the common law

---

[30] See the excellent note in the *Annual Practice 1973*, § 15/16/1.

system. When the administrative agencies of government intervene to support or regulate the life cycle of human beings in need or in trouble, their authority is statutory: the power to make binding declarations of right enables the court to declare in a proper case whether what is done is, or is not, in compliance with the statute. Since it is inconceivable that government would act contrary to law thus declared, the power represents an opportunity for the courts to exercise a very real measure of judicial control over the administration.

It is because these remedies exist, as well as for other reasons associated with the temper of the British people and the degree of their trust (and distrust) of civil servants and judges, that there is no popular movement for introducing into our legal system any institution of control of the administration comparable with the French Conseil d'Etat. The need for such an institution is not yet felt, and the civil service character of the Conseil d'Etat raises doubts in English minds. Yet reluctance to resort to an essentially administrative solution to a problem arising from essentially administrative activity must not blind us to the fact of the challenge. For the existence of the remedies is of no avail, and the challenge will not be met, if lawyers keep their distance from the apparatus which has to be controlled, while judges limit themselves to statutory interpretation.

The problem, therefore, is not—do the remedies exist? but—are the courts ready to develop the opportunity offered by them? It is a problem not merely of technique, but of legal policy. The obstacle not yet met, let alone surmounted, by English law is the extent to which the courts should question the justice of an administrative decision: put simply, can, or should, the courts assess the evidence, or lack of it, in determining whether to uphold, modify, or quash the decision? To this, the ultimate challenge of the welfare state, the law's response is still hesitant and confused—though there are indications that in commercial and financial fields, where also the state has intruded with its administrative agencies, the judges are ready to take the activist line, and intervene if there is no substantial evidence to support the administrative or tribunal decision, if the tribunal took into account a factor which they had no right to take into account.[31]

Nevertheless there continues to flourish an influential body of legal opinion which would confine the role of the courts and the general law to the interpretation of the statutes and the statutory instruments which are the legal framework of the system. By all means (the argument goes) let legal advice and assistance be available to help the citizen: but limit legal control to the task of confining the administrator and the appeal tribunal to their own field of activity as defined by statute. This view would exclude the ordinary courts, administering the general law, from reviewing the merits of a decision: it is as if lawyers are to be banned from refereeing the

---

[31] *e.g. Padfield* v. *Minister of Agriculture* [1968] A.C 997 and *Anisminic Ltd.* v. *The Foreign Compensation Commission* [1969] 2 A.C. 147.

match, though judges are to act as linesmen and practitioners may advise and cheer on the players. The significance of this way of thinking is great. Fundamentally it accepts that there may, indeed that there will, exist a world of rights and obligations not amenable to the control of the ordinary courts of the land. It solves the problem of public law by the expedient of leaving it alone so long as it does not trespass outside its territory. In other words, we are to have not one legal system but two or more. It is a retreat from the universality of the common law, and from the principle of one law. It leaves a vacuum, which will have to be filled: if the general legal system with its unifying appeal structure is kept separate from the " 52 plus " [32] categories of administrative tribunals, some substitute will have to be found. And, if not the courts, will we not be driven to some administrative solution—perhaps even an independent administrative body such as the Conseil d'Etat? The traditionalist attitude of averting the legal gaze from the movement of the beasts in the field (so long as they remain in the field) is, therefore, self-defeating. It means ultimately, that a new legal world (for the presence of right and obligation means it is that) will develop outside the control of the common law system. Here, then, is the challenge: the law does not lack the means to meet it, but is the legal profession willing to adjust its thinking and work out a socially-effective response? Have we lawyers the will? Time alone can show.

---

[32] Annual Report of Council on Tribunals, 1972/3 (May 1974).

PART IV

THE CHALLENGE OF THE ENVIRONMENT

FOR environment a traditional lawyer reads property: English law reduces environmental problems to questions of property. Establish ownership or possession and the armoury of the English legal cupboard is yours to command. This is not to say that English law is, or has ever been, helpless in face of a threat to the environment. Trespass and nuisance have proved over the centuries potent causes of action enforceable by the effectual remedies of injunction and damages; and, on occasion, the law permits self-help as well, *e.g.* in the abatement of nuisance by going on one's neighbour's land and rooting it out. But, as ever, the law operates only when set in motion by litigants with the necessary means and determination: for instance we owe to the determined use by anglers of the law of nuisance the arousing of national interest in the pollution of our rivers and the emergence of action to diminish it.[33]

Nor was the common law helpless in face of the threat to the environment presented by the industrial and technical developments of the nineteenth century, though it has to be conceded in retrospect that Parliament, not the courts, must be given most of the credit. I take two

---

[33] Sustained pressure by litigation or the threat of litigation was exerted by anglers upon local authorities, river boards, and industrial undertakings.

examples well-known to every law student, the development by the judges of a remedy in damages for damage
done to one's property by the non-natural use of land—
the familiar Rylands versus Fletcher principle—can be
seen as a significant attempt to protect the environment
against the consequences of industrial and technological
development. Like so many judicially-created rules, it
contains its own obscurities and raises new problems:
but the cynic may say that this is one of the strengths of
the common law. The illumination of obscurity and the
process of first asking and then, perhaps years later,
answering fresh questions has given, and still gives, the
law, and the judges, a degree of flexibility and the room
for manoeuvre, which in turn bring the gift of survival.
What is a non-natural use of land? Does what was un-
natural in a pre-industrial society become natural as the
technological revolution takes over? Does the principle
apply to personal injury or financial loss, as it admittedly
does to damage to property? These questions have
enabled the judges to flex their muscles, and their answers
have shown the common law adjusting itself with
ingenuity and a measure of success to a particular sort of
environmental threat. My second example is the development of the law of negligence. Its classic exposition is to
be found in the famous words of Lord Atkin:

> " . . . in English law there must be, and is, some
> general conception of relations giving rise to a duty
> of care . . . The rule that you are to love your neigh-
> bour becomes in law, you must not injure your

neighbour; and the lawyer's question, Who is my neighbour?, receives a restricted reply." [34]

The judges have done wonders with the principle of the duty of care. It lies at the root of the defences erected by judges and Parliament for the safety, health and welfare of society at work and play, in the factory, on the roads, and at home. As with the principle of strict liability, so also the principle of negligence has owed much of its value to its own inbuilt imprecisions and obscurities: they have given the judges the opportunity they needed to develop it to meet changing conditions.

But the truth has to be faced. The judicial development of the law, vigorous and imaginative though it has been, has been found wanting. Tied to concepts of property, possession, and fault, the judges have been unable by their own strength to break out of the cabin of the common law and tackle the broad problems of land use in an industrial and urbanised society. The challenge appears, at this moment of time, to be likely to overwhelm the law. As in the area of the social challenge, so also the guarding of our environment has been found to require an activist, intrusive role to be played by the executive arm of government.

The state with its money and managers has marched into an area where until the last hundred years it was unknown. At first it used the existing legal system. The Factory Acts, which the courts have interpreted as giving a right to damages to an employee injured by their breach,

---

[34] *Donoghue* v. *Stevenson* [1932] A.C. 562, 580.

are an illustration of the early intrusion. But they brought with them an inspectorate, the exercise of whose discretion lies outside the effective control of the law. The Factory Acts have, therefore, fallen between two stools and are themselves suspect today. Should they be concerned at all with financial compensation for injury? Should not their object be, to the exclusion of all else, the maintenance of safety and health at work? They have been used by the legal profession and the courts for one purpose, by the inspectorate for the other. In so far as they have been latched on to the common law by the lawyers, they are a compensation code operating only indirectly to protect the environment: in so far as they have been concerned directly to protect the workers' environment, the inspectorate has relied almost exclusively on extra-legal action, remaindering the law to the abnormal situation of prosecution when all else has failed.[35]

But the Factory Acts have had other, very serious consequences for the common law. They have cast a shadow upon the whole system of compensation for fault. Is the factory the only environment in which man should be entitled to the remedy of damages, *i.e.* full compensation notwithstanding his inability to establish any fault on the part of another? True, he has to prove a breach of statutory duty, *i.e.* a breach of the Factory Acts: but such breaches frequently occur without fault or negligence on the part of the factory owner. If a safe environment be seen, as increasing numbers of people

---

[35] See Law Commission Working Paper 1970, No. 30.

now regard it, as one of our human rights, why should compensation be available only to those who are fortunate enough to have the evidence to prove fault on someone's part? Yet, why should some other person (or his insurance company) pay if there be no fault? These questions, as is well known, are being considered by a Royal Commission under Lord Pearson. Their relevance to my theme is that the law, left to itself, cannot solve them. New principles will have to be accepted, old concepts and classifications discarded: and everywhere room will have to be found for the busy, intruding government deploying its money and its managers. Will they be subject to effective control within the general legal system, or will some extra-judicial, administrative control take its place?

Modern man demands not only a safe and healthy but a pleasant and economically viable environment. He sees this as a human right independent of the ownership or possession of property. Individually, men have relied on the acquisition of property to protect their environment. But the property law, the most elaborate, and if I may say so, without offence, the most astonishing creation of the English legal profession,[36] cannot meet the modern requirement. If land were always to be controlled by land owners who were enlightened and prepared to plan their land use with an eye to the needs of the unborn generations, the law could do an excellent job:

---

[36] "One of the most brilliant creations of English law," *The Rational Strength of English Law*, F. H. Lawson (London, 1951) (Hamlyn Lecture).

easements, long leases, restrictive covenants, stand as historical monuments to the law's endeavour to meet the wishes of land owners eager to protect the environment of themselves and their families. Since the land owner's environment is part and parcel of that of the rest of us, his protection happens also in some respects to be ours. But it has proved not to be enough. A bad land owner could not be prevented from doing irreparable harm: and there were interests besides those of the environment which the law had to accommodate—freedom to buy and sell, to develop, and to use one's own property as one wished. In the clash of interests which the law had to reconcile there was one major casualty—society's interest in land use. This interest the law could not directly protect, because of its starting-point in the law of property. And so, beginning in 1909,[37] came the now familiar sequence of Town and Country Planning legislation. But this legislation achieved little until 1947, when the real break with the legal system came. In that year the Town and Country Planning Act was enacted, ensuring that no one could thereafter ignore or avoid government policy in the use of land. Any material change in the use of land required planning permission from the local planning authority: county councils and county boroughs were required to prepare and publish development plans, the object of which was to establish the policy for land use in their areas. The citizen who found himself denied

---

[37] Part II of the Housing, Town Planning etc. Act 1909: Pt. I, significantly, was concerned with the "Housing of the Working Classes."

planning permission could appeal on the merits only to the Minister. Citizens were also entitled to raise objections to a development plan which affected them and their objections were to be considered by the Minister before he approved or modified the plan. The machinery established for hearing appeals and objections was the local public enquiry conducted by an inspector, who was the Minister's man—appointed by him, reporting to him. The Minister was free to accept or reject, in whole or in part, his inspector's report. In the early days the citizen never saw the report—but only the Minister's decision: that has now been changed and the report is normally made available. The inspectors, who over the years have earned the respect of the professional lawyers and surveyors who attend their enquiries and read their reports, are not lawyers, but are usually drawn from the architects, surveyors, and, less frequently, the civil engineering professions: by now, many of them have a qualification in the new profession of Town and Country Planning. It would be unreal to pretend that the public has anything like the same confidence as the professionals have in the merits and justice of the local public enquiry. The inspector lacks the independence and power of a judge in his court: the public are only too well aware that he does not make the decision: they feel they are never face to face with whoever it is—Minister or civil servant— who does. The law is kept at arm's length from the process: it is there only to ensure that the statute, and the statutory rules for conducting the process, are obeyed, but is not concerned with any of the problems of land use with which the process has been established to deal, and which are the problems that interest the citizen.

The Town and Country Planning legislation is, therefore, a code regulating land use largely by extra-legal means. It goes much further than the practice of compulsory acquisition of land with which our society has become increasingly familiar since the middle of the nineteenth century. Compulsory purchase of land by a public authority for a specific purpose defined by statute has emerged as the legal weapon for changing the environment, *e.g.* constructing a railway, road, or airport, building a school, clearing a slum, or comprehensively redeveloping a decayed urban area.[38] It is an important instrument in the hands of the state for the development and protection of our environment and, like planning control, is subject to the process of the local public enquiry, and only marginally subject to any direct legal control: the merits of acquisition are kept away from the courts. Nevertheless, compulsory acquisition remains the exceptional case: but planning control of land use is universal, affecting the citizen in the every day use of what belongs to him.

In the protection of our environment as in the provision of social security, government with its money and managers has moved, a welcome intruder, into the empty spaces of the law. Dirigism has never been a feature of the common law: on the contrary, it has been regarded as a theory and a practice likely to undermine freedom. But, faced with new problems and accepting a new scale

---

[38] See *Statutes in Force, sub tit.* " Compulsory Acquisition."

of values near the top of which one finds such newly-formulated freedoms as the " Roosevelt freedoms " from want, poverty, and disease and a whole new code of human rights, society has decisively accepted the dirigist activities of government in the use of land, a field of the law hitherto dominated by private property and private right. Thus the protection of the environment has come to be another administrative task undertaken by the executive arm of government. The common law concepts of trespass and nuisance, being rights of action available to the owner or occupier of land, the founding of rights upon property and possession, and the elaborate apparatus of the property law with its easements, restrictive covenants, long leases, and building schemes have failed because they have been ultimately no more than means for protecting private right and enforcing private obligation: the law has never understood or accommodated a public right or obligation in the environment save, perhaps, for the right of passage along the King's highway. Society has now broken into this private world of land ownership, and for the moment its weapons are administrative and extra-legal. When analysed, the challenge is similar in character to the social challenge, raising the same, so far unanswered questions. The law can now be directed along one of two routes. The problems of the environment can be left to administrative control or an attempt can be made to use the legal system so as to ensure that the merits of decisions taken are subject to a measure of review. The difficulties in reconciling the requirements of the policy with effective legal principle should not be allowed to obscure the fact that there are rights to be supported, obligations to be enforced, in a conflict between citizen and government over land use. It is a world of law as well as of administration, and there is a requirement for the rule of law as well as for the implementation of policy. How is the needed regulation of conflict to be provided—by the legal system as we know it, or by some specialist system, administrative in emphasis and remote from the general law? If the law and lawyers are to retain a relevant role in environmental law, they must find an answer to these questions. And it must be an answer which society finds helpful.

PART V

THE INDUSTRIAL AND REGIONAL CHALLENGES

(a) *The Industrial Challenge*

IT is perhaps not surprising that these two essentially political challenges to the legal system are as formidable as any. One is actual, and one potential. The first is the industrial challenge, already with us, and currently unanswered: the other, the constitutional challenge, has broken the horizon with the growth of nationalism in the countries that together make up the United Kingdom and with the publication of the Report of the Royal Commission on the Constitution.[39] In a judge discretion is the better part of valour: I shall, therefore, say little about the repeal of the Industrial Relations Act 1971, and nothing about the legislation which has replaced it. But the chaos and confusion that has been endemic in industrial relations for many years are not to be disregarded in the context of my argument.[40] Everyone agrees, I hope and believe, that an appropriate place has to be found for industrial relations within the law. The question not yet resolved is: where is that place to be? More specifically, we have not yet decided whether industrial relations are to be regulated in accordance with a law interpreted and applied within a unified legal system,

---

[39] Cmnd. 5460: the Kilbrandon report.
[40] For a description, see the "Donovan" report: Cmd. 3623.

or "extra-legally," *i.e.* in accordance with some specialised system of control isolated from the general legal system. If we opt for the latter, there are, I suggest, two likely consequences. First, we shall be witnessing yet another move away from a general legal system to specialised and detached systems—a trend already to be detected in current attitudes to common market law, the social security system, and the regulation of land use: secondly, there will arise a real risk of forces of great power in our society escaping from the rule of law altogether. Such consequences, if they ensue, would, there can be no doubt, constitute a weakening of the capacity of law to impose restraint on the exercise of power in society. The Industrial Relations Act 1971 was an attempt to subject the power of the trade unions to the rule of law as interpreted and applied by a court forming part of the general legal system of the land. The unions have overthrown it. It does not, however, follow that because this piece of legislation has proved to be unavailing and unacceptable the case for the rule of law in industrial relations is unsound. What is clear is that the general legal system conceived as one based on common law principles has not proved an acceptable instrument of control: but the need for control, and control according to law, will remain so long as men believe that uncontrolled power is an evil to be eradicated from civilised society. The challenge which faces lawyers is to win and retain public confidence in the law as the instrument of control. I say no more of industrial relations than that the failures of the law point the need not for

the rejection, but for the reappraisal, of the legal system:
only if the reappraisal fails to produce an acceptable
answer, should we embark on the unknown, but deeply
suspect, waters of a vital human activity developing
outside the control of the general law.

(b) *The Regional Challenge*

I turn now to the potential challenge of the nationalist
movement within the United Kingdom and the implications for the legal system of the report of the Royal
Commission on the Constitution.[41] This tremendous
document is, in truth, not one report, but two. Neither
the majority nor the minority report has much to say
about the law. The majority report really assumes that
devolution by Parliament of some of its legislative
powers upon regional assemblies will create no significant problems for the law: and it discounts the importance of the Common Market. Lord Crowther-Hunt and
Professor Peacock, the authors of the minority report, do
recognise the existence of legal problems, and indeed,
foresee opportunities for legal development ahead. Legal
difficulties do not disappear merely because they are not
discussed: and I am going to suggest that, if devolution
or some system of legislative independence for the
regions of the United Kingdom is to come (as now
seems certain), difficulties will arise and society could be
greatly benefited by making use of the law and the power
of the judges. It is not my intention to discuss the proposals of the Royal Commission in detail. Indeed I am

---

[41] Cmnd. 5460.

concerned with its two reports only in so far as they recommend a measure of devolution of legislative power to regional or national assemblies within the United Kingdom. Both reports reject a federal solution. Those members of the majority who recommend " legislative devolution " really propose something close to what became the constitution of Northern Ireland under the Government of Ireland Act 1920. " Power would be transferred to the regions to determine policy on a selected range of subjects, to enact legislation to give effect to that policy . . . while reserving to Parliament the ultimate power to legislate for the regions on all matters." [42] Control of the regional assemblies would be by the power of the central government (exercisable, perhaps, only with the approval of Parliament) to veto " unacceptable " regional legislation. The minority, apart from showing a more lively appreciation of English grievances than the majority (who really contemplate regional assemblies for Scotland, Wales and Northern Ireland, but not England), make more radical proposals. They would concentrate the work of the central Parliament upon questions of general policy, international affairs, and the Common Market, and transfer the detailed implementation of policy and a wide range of specific administrative and financial powers to elected area assemblies, of which they propose seven for the various regions of the United Kingdom. They foresee the possibility of legal conflict, and comment that " unless proper controls and procedures are followed, it could

[42] Cmnd. 5460, para. 733.

result in two highly undesirable consequences: (A) it could produce a very large amount of litigation where an ordinance might be thought to be in conflict with a United Kingdom statute ... ; (B) policies adopted by a particular Area government might have ... unacceptable repercussions on neighbouring areas or for United Kingdom policies generally." [43]

Somewhat optimistically—or so it seems to me—they think that these consequences can be obviated by a requirement of prior approval by the United Kingdom government to an area's " proposed ordinances ": I fear that this requirement would turn out to be either a cipher or a factor making for deadlock. Nevertheless the minority does attach greater importance to the law than does the majority: they comment that there may be a case for setting up a constitutional court and they see value in a Supreme Court of Appeal "from all our various administrative tribunals." They take these possibilities no further, suggesting that they should be " determined in the light of our actual experience of the consequences of Common Market membership and of the operation of the intermediate level governments," i.e. their area administrations which they see as interposed between central and local government. [44] Thus neither the majority nor the minority recommends changes in the legal system (or systems) of the United Kingdom, though both implicitly recognise that there are legal difficulties underlying their proposals. In a

---

[43] Cmnd. 5460–1, para. 221.
[44] Cmnd. 5460–1, para. 308.

passage on human rights [45] the majority recognises that there is an argument for curbing the sovereign power of the supreme legislature by use of the courts to determine "constitutional limits," though they clearly do not appreciate the extent to which our international obligations (the Common Market and human rights) have already propelled us in this direction. The minority, as I have already said, does see the legal problem and the opportunities it offers for developing the law.

I go so far as to submit that it would be irresponsible to initiate constitutional change without legislating for its legal implications. Unfortunately the emphasis of the English common law and, if I may be so bold as to say so, of Scots law also, upon private law, and the lack of any developed public law encourage the formulation of proposals upon the basis that one need consider neither the problems nor the value of developing our legal system to strengthen and assist the proposed new constitution. There is here a blind spot in legal thinking for which we common lawyers are largely to blame.

First, is the Royal Commission justified in minimising the importance, or postponing indefinitely the consideration, of the legal problems? I think not. Problems of two sorts are sure to arise. First, as between the regional and central legislatures. It is said that very few such problems arose during the 50 years of the Stormont Constitution. But there is no parallel here: Stormont, backed by a majority of Northern Irish public opinion, was desperately anxious, up to the very moment of its

---

[45] Cmnd. 5460, pp. 228–231.

suppression, to foster links with the United Kingdom.[46] It would be surprising, given the current trends of Scottish and Welsh national feeling, if an Edinburgh or Cardiff assembly would be as enthusiastic for the link with London as was Belfast for 50 years. Such assemblies may reasonably be expected to explore the extent of their legislative powers and to seek the independent arbitrament of the courts if they find themselves at variance with the central Parliament in the interpretation of the extent of their powers. Inevitably, therefore, legislative devolution will bring with it a role for the courts: and it will be a role similar in character to that which, under the guidance of the European Court of Justice, has to be assumed by the courts when faced with a question as to the validity of Community legislation. Secondly, there is the impact of all this new elaborate, complicated machinery of government upon the citizen. If " Kilbrandon "—majority or minority version—is implemented, we shall be the most governed off-shore islands in the world—more especially when you add for good measure Brussels as well. As the Commission recognises, there will be a severe problem as to how to ensure equal social, economic, and personal rights throughout the *de facto* independently governed regions of the United Kingdom. It will also be necessary, for the reasons already given, to ensure that everyone in every region of the United Kingdom enjoys the human rights declared in international instruments to which the United Kingdom

---

[46] This significant feature is recognised in the majority report: see Cmnd. 5460, para. 556.

is a party. Moreover these citizens' rights must be safeguarded not only against administrative or executive tyranny but against the ambitions, the excess of zeal, and sometimes the prejudice or panic, of the central and regional legislatures. Where else in the plethora of these new law-making bodies will one find an independent arbiter capable of declaring and enforcing the rights of the citizen than in the courts?

To sum up, the Kilbrandon report contains a challenge, no less real because it is not expressly stated, to lawyers to provide a solution within the law of the conflicts between legislature and legislature, and between citizen and government. The common law system with its un-conditional subservience to the latest enacted word of Parliament cannot do the job. But, if we were to take constitutional law away from the corridors of Parliament and to insist that there should be a public and constitu-tional element in the legal system, it should be possible to ensure that even legislatures were subject to the rule of law. It is perhaps too often forgotten that one of the merits of the rule of law is that it is a curb upon power— irrespective of the person or institution who wields it.

Part VI

THE WARNING

Such are the challenges, or some of them, to our established legal system. What are the warnings—urgent
warnings I suggest—that the challenges I have considered are passing to the lawyers, be they judges, practitioners, or teachers? First, if human rights are to be
protected in a manner consistent with our international
obligations, some means other than the common law
must be found. A legal system at the mercy of a legislature, which is itself, save in a minority situation, at the
mercy of the executive, is no sure guarantee of human
rights. For the same reason, legislation, by itself, affords
no greater safety: what is needed is that the law should
protect the legislation. Thus the human rights movement,
which is now not merely a campaign but a matter of
international obligation, reveals the basic imbalance of
our constitution, and points towards the need for a new
constitutional settlement. Without a Bill of Rights protected from repeal, amendment, or suspension by the
ordinary processes of a bare Parliamentary majority controlled by the government of the day, human rights will
be at risk: " Of what assurance is a law to prevent so
great an evil, if it be in the same legislature to unlaw it
again? " [47] The significance of the Common Market is
that it shows already to exist a constitutional departure

[47] p. 17, *supra.*

by English law from the basic common law pattern. Within the defined, but ever broadening, range of activities covered by the European Treaties, the imbalance of power between courts and legislature has been redressed: not only is Parliament's "absolute" legislative sovereignty an anachronism so long as the Treaties are part of our law, but the legislative organs of the European Community (the Council of Ministers and the Commission) are subject to the legal control of the European Court of Justice charged with ensuring that the Treaties are observed: and the treaties are themselves entrenched constitutional provisions capable of being modified only by unanimity. The international challenge, therefore, does more than point to the need for a new constitutional settlement: it shows the law and the constitution already moving towards one.

When one turns from the international to the internal scene the same lesson emerges. A legal system, which offers only distributive justice, has been found wanting. A law of torts, a land law, and a family law, conceived on common law principles however admirable in substance, cannot effectively protect the general public or the weak, the poor, the aged and the sick. To satisfy the conscience of the nation the state has had to move into the empty spaces of the law, the deserts and hill country left uncultivated by distributive justice, and there to make provision for society as a whole, and for those not strong enough to provide for themselves. Thus the welfare state is challenging the relevance, or at least the adequacy, of the common law's concepts and classifications. Fault, trespass, property, even marriage, are now seen to be an insecure base for the development of a law suited to the needs of our society. Family life has been freed from the tyranny of the husband and its obligations buttressed by the state: social security is available on the basis of need and as of right: the use of land, sea and air are controlled in the interests not of property but of society anxious to protect its environment: and in these developments there is a diminishing role for the common law, the common lawyers, and the courts. The law is being remaindered—but to what? To death in a forgotten corner? or is there a new role? Lawyers use a technical term to describe this field of battle—administrative law: and English lawyers tend to treat its problems as technical, *i.e.*, the interpretation of statutes and the strengthening of the remedies available to the citizen against the executive arm of Government. But this is no merely technical problem amenable to a tinker-tailor approach for its solution. Our legal structure lacks a sure foundation upon which to build a legal control of the beneficent state activities that have developed in this country. But, though we find here, as with the international challenge, a strong case for a new appraisal and a new settlement, the welfare state poses further questions. As the traditional business of the civil courts falls away (a movement which is inevitable as the importance of merely distributive justice diminishes), the business of the so-called administrative tribunals, which guard the citizen where the administrator has taken over from the law, is certain to increase. Unless the legal profession adjusts its practice to this new forensic world, its own place in society will become unsure, and the relevance of law and lawyers to the solution of modern problems suspect.

Should this happen, there would be little value in discussing the technical questions of administrative law: society would quietly move from the constitutional position of legal control to one of administrative control, tempered no doubt by administrative safeguards such as an ombudsman (or a whole series of ombudsmen), or by a body such as the Conseil d'Etat of France. The welfare state poses, therefore, more than one difficult question for lawyers and the law: but it undoubtedly also points, like the other challenges, to the need for a new constitutional settlement that would fill the gaps and make good the omissions of the existing common law system.

The two political challenges reinforce the message. In industrial relations there is a powerful, and for the present apparently successful, movement away from legal control within a unified general legal system to some form of highly specialised regulation outside the law. The Report on the Constitution envisages the granting of a measure of legislative independence to national or regional assemblies within the United Kingdom subject to checks operated not by legal process in the courts but politically and administratively—politically by conferring a power of veto on the central Parliament and administratively by the extra-legal, civil service device of an ombudsman, though the minority does contemplate the possibility of a constitutional court.

Assessed in the aggregate, the implications of all these

challenges are serious. They suggest that the legal system has been found inadequate to handle the major issues arising in our society, and they show proposals being implemented for the extra-legal management and control of social security, the environment, industrial relations, and the constitution. By and large, lawyers and the legal system will be left to handle the criminal law and the private disputes of citizen and citizen: public law is to remain an exceptional activity limited to demarcation disputes arising on the meaning of statutory provisions and to the exercise of a restricted measure of control over inferior judicial bodies. The universality of the law—which is where the common law started—would be discarded: our rights and liberties would depend, and our obligations would be declared and defined, by complex governmental machinery, subject not to the rule of law administered by the ordinary courts but to administrative and political controls, themselves beyond the reach of the law. A system, or set of systems (for in truth unity would have disappeared) administratively and politically controlled could, no doubt, in this age of technological computer devices and rapid communications, be made to work: but where are the safeguards against power? The men who press the buttons would be the very same men as those who manipulate the Parliamentary majority—which, once legal control is remaindered to a tiny forgotten corner of the edifice, is the only safeguard left. Acute problems will arise between the citizen and the system: are we content that they should be resolved by the men who operate the system? A reformed rule of

law should be able to offer an answer. Restraint on power
and the avoidance of anyone, even a Parliamentary
majority or the men who possess it, being ultimately
judges in their own cause are the beginning of justice:
and it is justice that is at risk, as one dismantles or rele-
gates to a corner its familiar and well-tried processes—
simply because the substance of the law is inadequate.

To conclude, the common law system is in retreat: it
is being remaindered to corners of the house which are
unvisited by most members of society. The basis of the
system is not only challenged: it is being abandoned. Yet
the rule of law must be preserved if we are to have a
just society. The problem, I have sought to argue, is not
technical but fundamental. The common law system is
part of our constitution: a new settlement is needed,
which will retain its strengths, while eradicating its
features of weakness and obsolescence. In times past the
strength of the common law was its universality together
with its origin in a customary law which owed nothing
to the legislative activity of Parliament; indeed, it preceded it. This strength, when ranged alongside the power
of Parliament, gave it victory over the King in the
seventeenth century and led to the constitutional settlement of 1688–1689. But the true victor in that settlement
was Parliament, whose sovereignty then began. Today,
however, it is Parliament's sovereign power, more often
than not exercised at the will of an executive sustained by
an impregnable majority, that has brought about the
modern imbalance in the legal system. The common law
is no longer the strong, independent ally, but the servant

of Parliament. This, perhaps, did not matter quite so much so long as the constitution of Parliament itself contained effective restraints upon the will of a bare majority in one House. The Parliament Act 1911 was, no doubt, a valuable democratic reform: but it did remove from our constitution an important check on legislative power and introduce an imbalance at its very centre—an imbalance which, if no redressing factor be found or devised, could well prove to be the precursor of further freedoms from restraint to be enjoyed by a bare majority in the Commons. I suggest that the less internal control Parliament is prepared to accept the greater the need for a constitutional settlement protecting entrenched provisions in the field of fundamental human rights, and the universality of the rule of law. Thus the lesson I think we lawyers have to learn from society's current challenge to the law is both negative and positive. On the negative side, we can no longer rely on distributive justice, concepts of property and individually owned rights, judge-made law, the adversary system, and a legal profession historically educated, if the rule of one law—the great blessing of the common law—is to be retained. On the positive side, we must seek a new constitutional settlement that makes use of judicial power to keep within constitutional limits the legislative sovereignty of Parliament, and to use the rule of law in resolving the conflicts that will arise between the citizen and the state in the newly developed fields of administrative-legal activity upon which the quality of life in the society of the twentieth century already depends.

PART VII

THE NEW DIMENSION

IT is not enough to diagnose an ill: I therefore, though with diffidence, will suggest a course of treatment.

First, the new constitutional settlement. This can, and should, take time. Once the policy is accepted, the programme of its implementation should be phased over a period of years. It need not begin with a constituent assembly or have as its objective a constitution written in one document or set of documents. Freeing ourselves of the conceptuality of the common law system, we should be on guard against falling prey to the conceptual thinking of others. Parliament is the assembly to put through the programme: and Parliament, uninhibited by current conventions, should consult others: for example judges, Scottish and Welsh nationalists, Ulster Unionists, trade unionists, and the many others, representative of the strands in our complex society and administration. All of us can, and should help to participate not only in the formulation of policy but also in the essential committee work. First on the agenda should be the problem of checks and balances to be imposed on the legislative sovereignty of the central parliament, and on the legislative power of the regional assemblies, if they come. I would expect that we would find ultimate sovereignty remaining with the central Parliament but the need for a substantial majority (*e.g.* two-thirds) to repeal or amend certain entrenched provisions. I would expect the entrenched provisions to include a Bill of Rights guaranteeing fundamental human rights, the European treaties, the devolution to regional assemblies, and the requirement for a statutory majority of substantial size before entrenched provisions could be touched. I would hope that a supreme court of the United Kingdom would be established (we already have its embryo in the judicial committees of the House of Lords and Privy Council) with power to invalidate legislation that was unconstitutional and to restrain anyone—citizen, government, even Parliament itself—from acting unconstitutionally. Sir Edward Coke at one time, thought the courts had this power: Cromwell thought it " necessary to good government ": We today must surely see that without it the aspirations of our society, let alone the international obligations of the state, will not be fulfilled.

The second phase of the programme, which could begin contemporaneously with the first, should be a survey, wide-ranging and profound, of the balance in the legal system between judge-made law and statute. The old common law balance, with statute being not the general rule but the intruding exception not to be gainsaid save, perhaps, by the confining influence of a strict judicial interpretation, cannot survive into the new world where judges, upholding the law of the constitution, may have on occasions to resist, instead of obeying, the declared will of Parliament. The survey could be undertaken by the two Law Commissions using the well-established and successful technique of publishing a working paper

(its consultative document) to be followed by wide-ranging
(international as well as national) consultation. The Commissions should be specifically requested to conduct a
feasibility study of a programme for moving the law from
its present basis—customary law as declared by the
judges, supplemented and modified by statute—to a
statutory basis, *i.e.* a code or set of interlinking codes.
The Commissions should be requested to consider the
implications for statutory drafting and interpretation in
going over to a law grounded on statute.

While these basic studies were being undertaken, I
would expect Parliament (or the Law Commissions reporting to a Minister responsible to Parliament) to consider
the problems of administrative law and law reform. A
satisfactory solution to the problems of administrative
law is vital to the survival of the rule of law: for this is
the extensive area of social justice taken over from the
old law by the agencies and money of the welfare state.
If (to take examples from the specific challenges I have
discussed) injustice arises in the distribution of the benefits of the social security system or in the control of land
use in the interests of the environment, grievances will
multiply and, if there be no acceptable outlet, disorder
will be brought nearer home.

But, though the initial study can be done by the Law
Commissions, there is here (as always with law reform)
an on-going problem. We have to plan for continuing
development. Social security, the environment, housing,
public transport, industrial relations (" the right " to a job
with acceptable pay and upon acceptable conditions, and,

perhaps, the worker's right to participate in the control and management of the enterprise in which he is employed) will pose new questions of administration and legal control: they will need, I suggest, continuous review. The Council on Tribunals, by extension of its membership and terms of reference, could become a suitable body for the on-going study necessary to keep the legal implications of this development in mind and manageable. The substantive law also calls for on-going study. Law is in constant need of review: like an urban centre, it becomes obsolete if it be not renewed. The common law has survived thanks to a measure of inbuilt capacity for change arising from its nature as judge-made. But this degree of flexibility, being erratic, confined to a view of the role of law in society which is no longer adequate for society's needs, and too much dependent on the length of the judge's foot, has failed to avoid the law's present disarray and its exposure to the risk of supersession by other remedies and other ways of getting done what society wishes done.

It is, therefore, vital to ensure that the new statute-based law should be fitted with its own machinery for law renewal, repair, and reform. There are two ways in which this can be done—both of them already in existence. The first is the judicial power of interpretation; the judge, treating statute no longer as the exception but as the basis of the law, will have to adopt the interpretative policy for which Lord Denning was once rebuked by Viscount Simonds—the policy of making good the omissions of Parliament consistently with the legislative purpose of the enactment.[48] The judge must be given a much wider discretion than he has now in the choice of evidence from which to infer the intention of Parliament: and he will have to free himself from the rigidities of *stare decisis* if he is driven to the conclusion that a previous decision, which he would normally treat as binding, misinterpreted the intention or meaning of Parliament. These greater powers—startling though they may appear in the context of the existing law—will be fully consistent with the new role assigned to the judges as guardians of the constitution. A bare majority of Parliament may seek to tinker with an entrenched provision: if so, the judges must have the means to see what is happening and to declare it void—a power that becomes more, not less, necessary, as the restraining power of the second chamber of Parliament diminishes.

The second way of ensuring the maintenance of the law's modernity is to use the Law Commissions for continuing review. Established by statute in 1965, the Commissions already have the necessary statutory powers. Their functions are thus described by the statute:

> " to take and keep under review all the law ... with a view to its systematic development and reform, including in particular the codification of such law ... and generally the simplification and modernisation of the law." [49]

---

[48] The rebuke is in *Magor R.D.C.* v. *Newport B.C.* [1952] A.C. 189.
[49] Law Commission Act 1965, s. 3 (1). The Act established the Law Commission for England and Wales and the Scottish Law Commission.

Taking the Law Commission as my example, its members—appointed by the Lord Chancellor from the ranks of the judiciary, the practising and the teaching profession—possess independence and the right to initiate proposals, save only that the Lord Chancellor may veto a subject proposed for study as part of their programme. It has devised a working method,[50] which is highly successful, and has a highly qualified legal staff drawn from the young as well as the older members of the profession. It has developed a close working relationship with Parliamentary counsel, some of whom are on full-time detachment to the Commission charged with the task of drafting Bills embodying the Commission's recommendations. This body has the expertise, the independence, and the terms of reference to enable it to keep codified law under continuous review, to report to Parliament anomalies, defects, omissions, and obsolescences as and when they emerge, and to recommend measures for reform.

My tentative proposals are, therefore:

(1) A new constitutional settlement replacing that of 1689 to be worked out by Parliament, the judges, the Law Commissions, and the Government through a phased programme of study, research, and extensive consultation;

(2) The basis of the new settlement should be entrenched provisions (including a Bill of Rights), and

---

[50] Consultation by working paper: for a short description, see Law Com. 12, p. 3, the Second Annual Report of the Law Commission.

restraints upon administrative and legislative power, protecting it from attack by a bare majority in Parliament;

(3) A Supreme Court of the United Kingdom charged with the duty of protecting the Constitution: if regional devolution comes, the problems of competing legislatures could be handled by this court, which would be at the pinnacle of the ordinary courts of the land;

(4) An immediate study should be begun of the problems of codification coupled with the associated problems of statutory drafting and interpretation in the new context of entrenched provisions and codified law;

(5) Machinery should be established (its embryo exists in the Council on Tribunals and the Law Commissions) for handling the on-going problems of the law's development and reform, with especial reference to the problems of administrative law.

We have the institutions to do the work—Parliament, the Judicial Committees of the House of Lords and the Privy Council, the Law Commissions and the Council on Tribunals. Indeed, if, as I think we should, we decide to add this new dimension to the law, very little structural change will be needed in the legal systems of the United Kingdom and its associated islands (the Isle of Man and the Channel Islands). My proposals do not diminish the substance of the common law: they add new law where the old has failed or retreated: they are designed to fill a legal vacuum. They do involve the conferring of new powers upon the courts but, with one very important exception, do not require a new court, or a new court structure. The exception is, of course, the proposed

Supreme Court of the United Kingdom. This court could be created anew: or by adaptation of the Judicial Committee of the House of Lords or the Privy Council. It would have no original jurisdiction, being exclusively an appellate court. The power to declare invalid and to quash legislation as unconstitutional would be exercisable in England by the High Court and, I would expect, by the Court of Session in Scotland, and would be subject to appeal to the Supreme Court. The powers of supervision and, on occasions, intervention in the work of administrative tribunals would be similarly distributed. If, therefore, we have the will to add a public law dimension to our legal system, the necessary technical changes should present no very great difficulties, and could be encompassed within the existing court structure. The judicial function of the House of Lords would, however, need enlargement or supersession.

I will take two hypothetical cases to illustrate how I see the system working. An unpopular splinter group proposes to exercise their fundamental, *i.e.* constitutional, right of free-speech by a march and peaceable protest in central London. Other groups, whose policies are currently more acceptable, are determined to prevent or disorganise the march and protest. I will assume two variants. First is that the Home Secretary has statutory power to stop a specific march, if he thinks it may provoke disorder, and that he is prevailed upon to order the march not to proceed. The splinter group, under my proposals, would have the right to challenge the Home Secretary's order as unconstitutional. If they were able to satisfy a judge of the High Court that their preparations were peaceable in intention and went no further than the exercise of a human right protected by the constitution, the fact that others alleged they would be provoked into criminally violent counter-demonstration would not suffice to deprive the citizen, however unpopular his cause, of his constitutional right.

The second variant is that a frightened Parliament is panicked into legislation, enacted with less than the majority needed for amending the constitution, forbidding the public expression of the views of the group, even when their expression is done peaceably and there is no breach of the criminal law either committed or reasonably anticipated. In such a case the group could ask the court to declare the legislation unconstitutional and to quash it. In either case, a remedy would be available before or after the event—the whole legal apparatus of remedies (declaration, injunction, damages) being available.

My second hypothetical case is of a woman seeking a state pension upon the basis of her husband's National Insurance contributions, he having disappeared. She is unable to prove his contributions, though she can say that he was in regular work as a bricklayer for over 40 years: she does not know whether he was an employed man or on the lump and so self-employed, or whether he or his employers paid up his stamps, or at what rate of contribution, if they did. Suppose first that her claim is disallowed, neither she nor the National Insurance officer being able—or so they say—to offer any evidence as to the husband's contributions. If on appeal within the system (*i.e.* to Commissioner or other administrative tribunal) she fails, the ordinary courts will have the power to review the decision, to call for further discovery of documents, to assess the implications of a lack of documentary (or other) evidence, and to quash the decision if the evidence, or lack of it, shows that injustice was done. One could envisage a principle of public law developing under which, if a Government department responsible for keeping records could not satisfactorily explain omissions or defects in the documents produced, the citizen should have the benefit of the doubt—in the absence of evidence to the contrary *omnia praesumuntur pro bono civis*. No doubt this can be achieved, and may already have been achieved, within the existing administrative structure governing the payment of pensions.[51] But who can doubt that the citizen will be on surer ground, and the law in more independent hands, if an appeal along the lines suggested lies to the ordinary courts? Given the will, the task of incorporating a public law and a constitutional element in English law presents, therefore, no insuperable problems. My final question is, therefore, have we the will?

The answer lies with the legal profession. If, as a profession, we respond to the needs of society and show by our practice and thinking that we have a socially relevant and helpful contribution to make to the management and

---

[51] Lord Denning pioneered this principle, when exercising appellate jurisdiction in respect of war pensions: see *Starr* v. *Minister of Pensions* [1946] 1 K.B. 345.

regulation of our society as it prepares to enter the twenty-first century, we shall be wanted, and respected. Can we do it? First, the judges: they have behind them 800 years of the common law's independent existence during which they alone have been able to declare what is the common law. Society wishes to lose neither their independence nor their self-confidence. Society, if I read its movement aright, asks only that they transfer their traditional skills, spirit and attitudes from declaring a law, the basis and nature of which no longer suffices to meet society's need, to interpreting, and guarding against the abuse of power, a modern, statute-based, and more activist law. Society asks of the judges no more than that they be true to the ideals of Coke and Cromwell.

Secondly, the practitioners. Practice has to be reviewed, and its financing. The lawyer has always liked to think that he is the natural champion of the weak and the oppressed. The new law of the welfare state conferring rights upon that sector of society will be too often frustrated unless those who have rights enforce them. Policy and lack of money available for legal services in this new world of the law have combined to enfeeble the lawyer's response to a challenge which, though new, strikes a very familiar chord—the protection of the weak. If, as I believe now to be probable, policy is released and a measure of legal aid is made available in administrative tribunals, and if the legal aid scheme is extended along the lines indicated by the Legal Aid Act of 1972 [52] and

---

[52] Now reproduced in the consolidating statute, Legal Aid Act 1974.

enlarged in character so as to include the financing of representative or test actions where a question of principle or policy of genuine importance arises, the practitioner will have his opportunity.

Thirdly, and in the long term the most important, the teachers of law. The key to the survival of the rule of law as a living and socially relevant force is legal education. The nature, the purpose, and the implications of a law suited to the requirements of the society in which he will have to practice must be brought home to the student. The so-called " core " subjects required by the Council of Legal Education as a necessary part of a barrister's training are at present:

> contract, tort, criminal law, land law, constitutional and administrative law, equity and trusts.

Are they relevant, or are they in the list because of their historical importance? Significantly, a recent recruit to the list is administrative law. But what of the others? Contract, if studied in abstraction from the many various settings in which a consensus of wills is relevant, is no more than a generalised theory about the nature and consequences of agreement coupled with rules, dangerous if made the subject of abstract study, as to the meaning of words and phrases. Tort is a doctrine, or several doctrines, of civil wrong, a concept no longer of general relevance, though it will continue to be of great importance in certain specific fields, *e.g.* defamation and protection of persons and their property. The land law (as also equity and trusts), is based on property but should be considered in the much wider, and socially more significant, context of the law relating to our environment. The student should be encouraged to study the real legal problems of the day: are we to have one legal system or several? How are we to integrate the rule of law with the requirements of administrative policy? How are we to secure and enforce the rights of those who find themselves in a conflict situation with the State?

The common law has no specific answer to these problems, but its ethos of independence combined with its respect for the rights of the weak is a sound base from which to tackle them. I would say to all three branches of the profession: look to the new sources and fields of law and endeavour to retain the spirit of the old while abandoning habits of thought and action derived from a society that no longer exists.